The Digest Book of

DOWNHILL SKIING

by
Frank Covino

DBI Books Inc., Northfield, Illinois

ACKNOWLEDGEMENTS

Very special thanks to my wife, Marge, for helping me finish this and all the various projects I begin with the confidence of knowing she is there appreciating the effort. Thanks also to Steve Pisni and Air Canada and Hans Gmoser for bringing us back to the incomparable Bugaboos, and to Louis Robinson of David Travels for taking us to Lake Tahoe and for requesting our services again next spring.

ISBN 0-695-81320-X

TABLE OF CONTENTS

DEDICATION

This book is dedicated to my 8-year-old daughter, Cami, who can follow me down any slope, if she gives me a head start.

INTRODUCTION

THIS BOOK is not written for downhill racers. Ski racers number but a fraction of the men, women and children who are into the sport of downhill skiing. The following pages are directed toward that larger number of participating skiers—those who ski for recreation and pure aesthetic enjoyment. It is not only an instructional book, designed to supplement on-slope learning, but is an especially good primer for those who would teach themselves. If you are a beginner, or are at the intermediate level of the learning process, you will find a complete ski education plus a prescription for physical fitness between these covers. However, the author is first to admit that no amount of reading can surpass the critical training that is available from qualified ski instructors on the slopes. You are advised to practice the exercises outlined in Chapters 1 and 3 with diligence and perseverance, (tuck this book into your parka!) but supplement your pragmatic self-education with an occasional class or private lesson at your favorite ski area in order to have your faults pointed out and corrected. Can you strengthen your body and learn how to ski with proficiency in one season? Read these words from just one of the letters in our file which is bursting from responses to Chapter 3, No Frills Ski Instruction, from Frank Covino's *Skiers Digest* Second Edition, DBI Books, Inc., Northfield, Illinois:

" . . . your book is nothing less than excellent. I respect and appreciate your philosophical approach to your students on a more individual basis . . . I started skiing without ever having been on skis before, and I must admit that I was skeptical. However, today I've progressed to the point where I can ski the advanced slopes of several ski areas in the competent style of my only instructor— Frank Covino.

I must add that I started this year with three others who began the same time as I but did not have the benefit of your direction, and I'm rather proud to say, with some modesty, that I have significantly surpassed their efforts and have even had the pleasure of one of them coming to *me* for some tips! . . . "

That was a small excerpt from the response of skier Tony Sposito of Winnipeg, Manitoba, Canada, whose one season of ski instruction was solely the review of the same instructional chapter (Chapter 3) we have repeated in this book, *The Digest Book of Downhill Skiing*, for your personal sports library. We are confident that it will benefit you as well.

The author skiing off the beaten path at Sunshine Village in Alberta, Canada. There are steeper grades for the intrepid.

Chapter 1

WEIGHT TRAINING FOR SKIING

TWENTY-FIVE YEARS ago, sports writers wondered how it could be physically possible for Olympic level athletes to ever surpass their already phenomenal physical achievements. Yuri Stepanov thought that only a special shoe could improve his high jump. After clearing 7 feet, 1-inch in Moscow in 1957, his "catapult shoes" were banned by the International Amateur Athletic Federation. Athletes in every sport seemed flawless and at the peak of human stamina; skiers like Stein Eriksen had seemed to find the perfect physical formula for maximum speed, grace and agility while tearing down a slalom course. If the performances of these athletes was to be exceeded, something in the physical make-up of new challengers had to be ameliorated—the equipment for the execution of their performances notwithstanding. Science, mathematics and advanced engineering offered sophisticated equipment for the athletes, such as the fiberglass pole for vaulting (as much as 2 feet could be added to bamboo pole records) and the more efficacious ski designs. But trainers were wise enough to realize that no matter how advanced the equipment, the primary force behind the achievement was *human* and that human force was dependent upon advanced physical and mental development. Enter the biomedics, nutritionists and psychologists.

Given two athletes who perform equally on the same equipment, say these physical scientists, how can we give athlete A the edge over athlete B, leaving athlete B in the dust at the next competition? Of course, their logical conclusion is to train the mind and body of athlete A beyond his or her current level of achievement, as the limitations of these mental and physical potentials are still distant mysteries. If, indeed, their performing equipment was the same, and both athletes undertook the same training for advanced development of these physical and mental potentials, the true human champion would be the victor and not the equipment with which he performed. In the area of physical development, weight resistance exercises were introduced to athletes of every sport. As their strength and endurance increased, their previous records were smashed and exceeded. In 1963, Valeriy Brumel exceeded the high jump record of Stepanov by 4¾ inches *without special shoes!*

I am always amused at the fanfare a driver in a Porsche receives when he wins another road race—would he have performed as well in a Ford? Who really is the victor, the man or the machine? Olympic contenders should be required to compete with the same equipment. Only then can the *human* victory be valid. The power of capitalist industry will never allow this, so *two* contests are being staged at any athletic event in which the competitor uses some form of equipment

for his performance; there is a mechanical and a human champion. The principal nationalistic effort is to bring the two together for Olympic competition.

The recreational skier can benefit from this dichotomous national competition. He can be rest assured that the brands of equipment which are furnished to the Olympic victors are made by quality companies which have designed effective equipment. Moreover, he profits from the competition between rival companies who are constantly challenging natural forces to produce the *most efficient* equipment for competition. These designs are passed down to their consumer line products. While you might not be purchasing the same set of skis designed for a champion, (and, don't kid yourself, high competition skis are specially modified to suit the needs of particular champions), the basic profile of recreational equipment made by a company with a good Olympic record is relatively consistent.

Most recreational skiers are aware of this, which can be attested simply by comparing the sales records of ski manufacturers. Serious recreational skiers equip themselves with the same brand of skis, boots and bindings that are used and touted by the champions. Look at the ads in the trade magazines. "Used by Hammerschwanze when he won his gold!" That sells skis. It is a pity that recreational skiers don't go farther in their analysis of what is required for maximum performance. Too many consider the tool and not the performer. A champion's capacities are written off as *talent*, and talent is considered something you are either born with or born without. The attitude is, "Well, I wasn't born a super athlete, but I can purchase equipment similar to what he is using and do as well or better than others who were born without talent . . . "

That kind of statement is a cop-out. I hear it on the slopes, and I hear it in my art school, and I can't help but think of the words of Benedetto Croce, Italian philosopher and author of *Aesthetic*, the science of beauty: "There are no born cooks, and there are no born poets." I believe that the human potential for mental and physical development has not nearly been realized. Super athletes are like scientists who have impressed us with the products of their highly educated minds. They are but examples of what each of us has the potential for becoming, given the same circumstances of exposure, training and environment. We must be at least subconsciously aware of this, else why would we be such a world of spectators? What football fan does not run vicariously with that receiver who streaks for the goal posts?

Participation sports, like recreational skiing, give the non-professional athlete a chance to perform rather than just dream of performing. Too often, the mistake he makes is in spending a fortune on equipment to achieve performance and then trying to participate with a body that isn't worth a dime. If his training is adequate, and his equipment is effective, he might even succeed with a mediocre performance, but a well-tuned body could make his performance superior.

Many letters were gratefully received by this office in response to our last edition of *Skiers Digest*. A surprising number of those responses came from readers who appreciated and practiced the body conditioning exercises I designed for that book which do not require resistance apparatus and which may be performed with an exercise partner. That course is still advised for pre-season conditioning and for maintenance on those days between ski weekends. Athletic readers, already in pretty good shape and eager to strive for maximum performance, have asked for more—an advanced course that would provide *more* periodic progressive stress exercises which would result in increasingly greater strength and endurance. Superior. This program will involve the use of weight resistance. I am convinced that proper administration of weight training, good nutrition and psychological insight has resulted in the phenomenal records that are currently being set by athletes today who compete at the Olympic level. Gone are the myths that used to cloud the practice of weight training with the stigma of narcissism. Exposed is the *secret* that all athletes can improve their performance at *any* sport with a properly administered program of weight resistance exercises. We have even become aware that the best shaped women in the world who can participate favorably in basic athletics also have been weight trained. I have qualified that last statement with a functional imperative because a well-shaped woman who can't perform is like a new car without a motor. My wife's recent book, *Woman's Guide to Shaping Your Body With Weights,* will convince you that women need not fear development of massive musculature when training with weights, unless their hormones are imbalanced (Fig. 1-1). The purpose of this program is not necessarily to develop Herculean men either, but is merely to give both sexes the edge in mastering the demanding sport of skiing with the least amount of effort. The course will bring you closer to the body you were intended to have and away from the aberration you might have developed from lack of sufficient exercise coupled with various forms of physical dissipation. The principal intention of this program is to make of you a better skier! My modest qualifications for administering this prescription are simply that I am 48 years old and am in top physical condition. I am certain that my skiing has benefited from the condition in which I keep my body, and my wife echoes my belief.

The Right and Wrong Way to Work Out

Many doctors and physical education directors have put down weight training as non-effective for cardiovascular conditioning because of the manner in which it has been practiced by body builders. The models for their studies were probably narcissistic weight lifters whose primary goal is hypermuscular development with little if any regard given to cardiovascular and muscular endurance. The recreational skier needs strength *and* endurance. Muscular development is a bonus. What you really want is to be able to boogie the bumps down a run like Al's at Taos without stopping for air or to massage a cramp.

Aerobic exercise primarily develops cardiovascular endur-

ance. An example of an aerobic exercise would be running— proper running. The jogger who boasts of doing his 2 miles a day is not properly conditioning his cardiovascular or respiratory systems unless he includes spurts of sprints, or runs uphill, running at maximum effort for sustained periods during his jog. That maximum effort should elevate his heart rate to a minimum of 75 percent of maximum stress. Your own maximum stress heart rate may be estimated by subtracting your age from the number 220. Thus, a 40-year-old's maximum heart rate would be 180 beats per minute (220 − 40 = 180). Seventy-five percent of 180 is 135. Jogging 2 miles may elevate the 40-year-old's heart beat to 120, but unless he includes sprints which get his heart to pump at 135 beats per minute for a sustained period, his cardiovascular and respira-

Fig. 1-1: Marge Covino proves that feminine curves can only be enhanced through proper training with weight resistance.

tory conditioning effort is lessened. That conditioning is your lifeline. Even the most muscular men die prematurely if they have not trained their cardiovascular and respiratory systems along with building up their massive muscles. This neglect has earned some weight lifters a low position on the longevity scale. Modern body builders and Olympic level athletes who train aerobicly with weights and watch their nutrition are the true supermen of today, and it is the wise athlete who has monitored their progress and borrowed their training methods to better his own performance at his chosen sport.

Training with weights in an aerobic manner can make you a better skier. Your strength and endurance will improve to an astonishing level. You will feel reborn. You can purchase some basic equipment for use in your own home or attend a local gymnasium. Before prescribing specific exercises, here are a few do's and don'ts.

DO'S AND DONT'S

DO begin every exercise period (and this includes your ski days) with 5 minutes of stretching and warm-up movements.

DO increase the amount of weight as soon as the tenth repetition becomes easy.

DO, for cardiovascular conditioning, begin every exercise with a warm-up set of 25-50 repetitions before performing the prescribed number of sets for muscular development.

DO alternate *one* arm or *one* leg exercises rather than two, in order to continue exercising the cardiovascular system with no rest. This keeps the heart rate up. Rest only 1 minute between each type of exercise and make this rest *active,* i.e. rapid walking.

DO employ a minimum of three sets for each exercise *after* a warm-up set with a lighter weight.

DO breathe deeply with every exercise, inhaling through your nose and exhaling through your mouth. Best is diaphragmatic breathing—the stomach moves *out* when in haling and *in* when exhaling.

DO practice peak contraction in every exercise (holding the position for a count of three when the working muscle is fully contracted).

DO practice negative tension (lowering or raising the weight very slowly after the moment of maximum effort).

DO work your body in a systematic direction (lower legs, followed by upper legs, followed by mid-section, then torso, neck and arms, etc.) to concentrate the blood in the area which demands the most immediate nourishment.

DON'T exercise with weights on days when you have skied vigorously. Good skiing taxes every muscle in the body and is sufficient exercise, particularly when some climbing is involved.

DON'T let your heart rate drop too low between downhill runs. Keep moving on the chair by swinging your skis and inventing isometric exercises (pitting one muscle against another or against an immovable object like the bar of the lift).

DON'T ever pick up a weight without warming up and stretching first.

DON'T use a weight that you can't handle for at least 10 repetitions. I suggest a minimum of 15 repetitions for all leg exercises.

DON'T exercise every day, unless you split your routine, working the arms and torso one day and the legs during the next. If the entire body is weight trained during one workout, you should follow with a day of rest for development and recuperation.

DON'T pick up a weight *of any poundage* without bending your knees and lowering your derrière.

DON'T pamper yourself. The last repetition should hurt and another repetition should be unbearable.

DON'T ever hold your breath during a lift. Closing the glottis is dangerous.

DON'T rest too long between sets. Active rest periods of 1 minute are best (walk around rapidly) to keep up the heart rate.

DON'T do too many sets with light weights. Fewer sets with maximum poundage is preferred. The *intensity* of the effort is more important than the duration for optimum development.

KNOW YOUR SKI MUSCLES

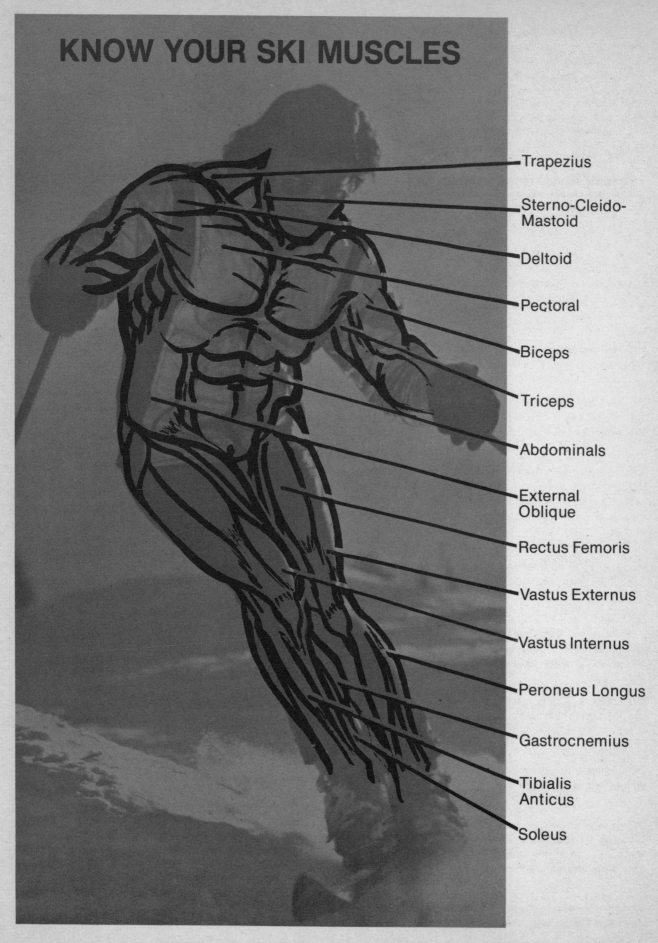

- Trapezius
- Sterno-Cleido-Mastoid
- Deltoid
- Pectoral
- Biceps
- Triceps
- Abdominals
- External Oblique
- Rectus Femoris
- Vastus Externus
- Vastus Internus
- Peroneus Longus
- Gastrocnemius
- Tibialis Anticus
- Soleus

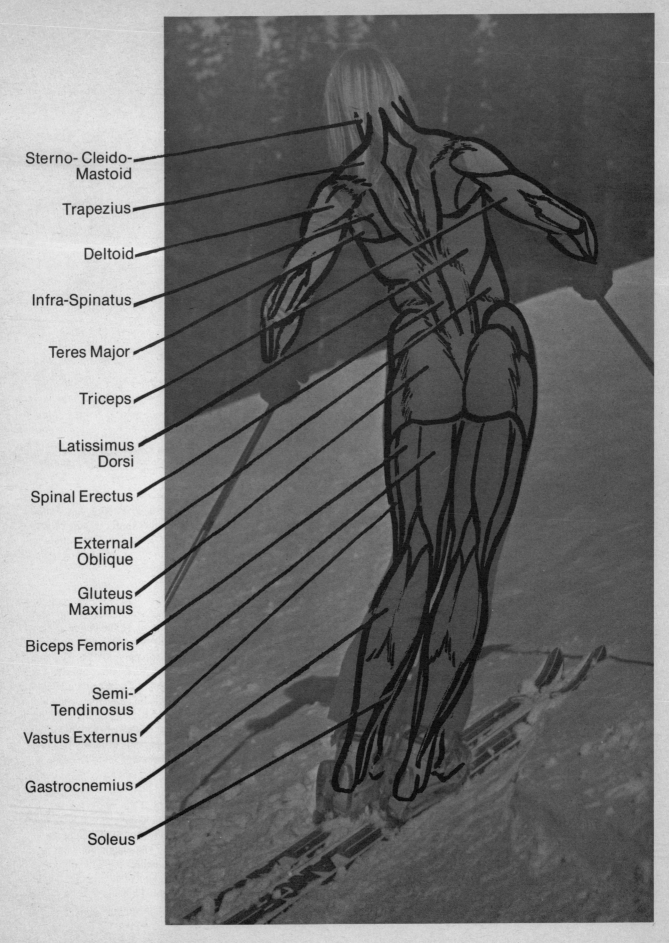

Sterno- Cleido- Mastoid

Trapezius

Deltoid

Infra-Spinatus

Teres Major

Triceps

Latissimus Dorsi

Spinal Erectus

External Oblique

Gluteus Maximus

Biceps Femoris

Semi- Tendinosus

Vastus Externus

Gastrocnemius

Soleus

Exercises

Each of the following exercises works on muscles and muscle groups. If you are not acquainted with the technical muscle names, e.g. "semi-tendinosis," and wish to know which muscle is being referred to and where it is located see pages 8 and 9 Know Your Ski Muscles.

Stretching and Warm-up Exercises: (Fig. 1-2)

You can invent these. Use any movement that will stretch and lightly exercise the body part that you will work with weights, before each exercise. An example would be a minimum of 50 Jumping Jacks just before working the calves with weights (Fig. 1-2). Without resting, proceed immediately to the first exercise.

Exercise 1: THE DONKEY LIFT (Fig. 1-3)

For this exercise, use an exercise partner for your weight resistance. A 3- or 4-inch board under your toes will allow a good stretch of both the gastrocnemius and the soleus muscles—what is normally called the *calf*. With your partner on your back, "piggy-back" style, lower your heels as far as they will go. Then stretch upward on your toes as high as you can and hold this contraction for a count of three. Do three sets of 15 repetitions. If your partner is too light, perform this

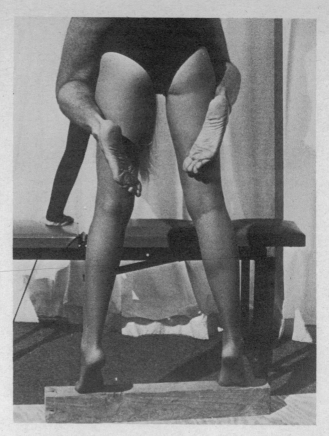

Fig. 1-3: DONKEY LIFT. Marge finds my 175 pounds the ideal weight for her legs. When we switch donkey roles, my daughter hops on my back with her.

Fig. 1-2: JUMPING JACKS. A very effective total body warm-up exercise. Marge shows the starting position. Leap high clapping your hands and land with feet spread apart. Then jump high and return to the first position.

exercise one leg at a time, with no rest in between. Performed with both legs, an active rest of no more than 1 minute should separate each set. Walking around rapidly would be sufficient "active rest." Perform an active rest when your sets are completed, then on to the next exercise.

Exercise 2: LEG CURLS (Fig. 1-4)

This exercise requires the apparatus seen in Fig. 1-4. You can find one at any good department store for under $50, or purchase a really good one from any reputable manufacturer of barbell equipment. They are not too ugly. We keep ours in our bedroom. From a fully extended prone position, curl the bar upward. You may warm up using both legs and a weight that you can handle for 25 repetitions. Increase the weight to a poundage that you can handle for 15 reps with one leg. Curl and hold the contraction for a count of three before lowering the weight slowly. Three sets of 15 with each leg (no rest between sets). Active rest for a minute, then on to Exercise 3.

Exercise 3: LEG EXTENSIONS (Fig. 1-5)

This exercise is performed on the same apparatus as you used for leg curls. Again, warm up with a light weight for 25 reps with both legs. Then, increase the weight for your one legged sets. From a flexed knee position, slowly raise your foot. Hold the contraction for a count of three, then lower slowly and repeat for 15 repetitions. Three sets, alternating with each leg. Active rest as before, then on to a great skiing exercise.

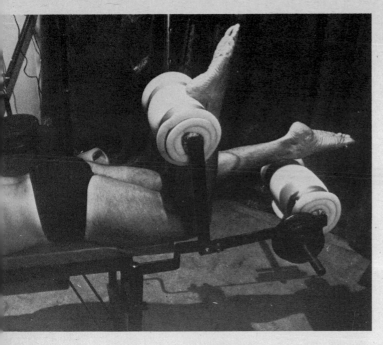

Fig. 1-4: LEG CURLS. Most gyms have an apparatus like this one, or if your wife doesn't mind, pick one up at your local sports shop and keep it in your bedroom. This is a dynamite exercise for bump skiers!

Fig. 1-6 (Above): HACK LIFTS 1 (with barbell). Hacks are by far the best leg exercise for skiers. Be sure to keep your heels on a high board or step and your back as straight and as vertical as you can.

Fig. 1-7 (Below): HACK LIFTS 2 (on the machine). You'll find one of these machines in any good health club or YMCA. I bought my machine from a barbell company. Look in your local Yellow Pages under gymnasium equipment. The machine puts less stress on the back.

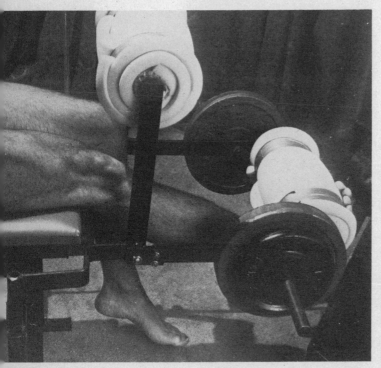

Fig. 1-5: LEG EXTENSIONS. Hold the contraction for a count of three before lowering the weight slowly.

Exercise 4: HACK LIFTS (Fig. 1-6 and Fig 1-7)

This is perhaps the most important weight training exercise for skiers, as it simulates the pumping movement required for unweighting on skis. This exercise strengthens your quadriceps which are the four major muscles on the front of your thigh—vastus externus, rectus femoris, vastus internus, and sartorius. You have the option of using a barbell as in Fig. 1-6,

Fig. 1-8 (Above): HAMSTRING STRETCH 1 (down). After a few repetitions, you should be able to touch the bar to the ground. Be sure to use a light weight to avoid stress on your back!

Fig. 1-9 (Right): HAMSTRING STRETCH 2 (up). Rise erect, chest out, chin up. Stretch the leg biceps sufficiently and you'll protect yourself from harm in a forward fall while skiing!

with your heels elevated on the same board you used for Exercise 1: The Donkey Lift (a rug draped over it would make it more comfortable), or you may prefer a "hack machine" like the one shown in Fig. 1-7, which you could purchase from any barbell company or find in any worthwhile gymnasium. Hold the barbell tightly and bend your knees until your thighs are parallel with the ground. Warm up the quadriceps with a fast set of 25 Hack Lifts, using a light weight. Then, increase the weight and perform three sets of 15. For each of these strength building sets, rise up and hold the contraction for a count of three, before lowering for another repetition. Keep your back as vertical as you can throughout the exercise. Remember, the last rep in each set should burn with effort. If it doesn't, increase the poundage.

Exercise 5: THE HAMSTRING STRETCH (Fig. 1-8 and Fig. 1-9)

This is a stretching exercise, more than a strength or bulk developer, and it may be used in place of your active rest period. Begin as soon as you have completed Exercise 4. Stand on a board that is at least 5 inches off the floor; a bench or chair will do. *Use a lightly weighted barbell.* If you haven't worked with weights before, the bar alone might be sufficient. The object is to hold the bar in front of your thighs, then lower it to your toes or lower, without bending your knees. I should repeat that the weight must be light if you are new to this form of exercise or you will risk a back injury. The movement should also be *slow.* On the first repetition, you might only get the bar midway between the knees and ankles, because most of us have shortened the hamstring muscles (biceps femoris and semi-tendinosus) from lack of full extension in our daily activities; particularly if we sit a lot. This is a form of muscle boundness that is quite common. If you *are* bound in that area, you risk a serious tear of the muscle or its tendon, should you take a forward fall with a poorly adjusted binding. Hold the position shown in Fig. 1-8 for a count of three, before rising to the posture shown in Fig. 1-9. Repeat for 15 repetitions, three sets, with active rest in between. Move on immediately to Exercise 6.

Exercise 6: SIDE BENDS (Fig. 1-11 and Fig. 1-12)

The hamstring stretching exercise provides the additional bonus of taxing the spinal erectus muscles, two columnar muscles shaped like elongated eels, which run up both sides of the spine from your sacrum to your trapezius, giving it necessary support. The exercise thus brings the capillary action upward from the legs to your midsection, in this sequential program. Now we will move the blood flow sideways to the external obliques—your side muscles—which come into play every time you angulate (Fig. 1-10). (Angulation is the optimum traversing posture at the completion of a turn, when the lower body tilts uphill and the torso tips downhill until the shoulders are parallel to the slope angle.) Fig. 1-11 is pretty self-explanatory. By placing your free hand on your head and spreading your legs, your right external oblique will be extended when you lower the weight and will be contracted when you rise to the position shown in Fig. 1-12. Hold this contraction for a count of three, before bending again. Fifteen repetitions, three sets, alternating each side with no rest in between. My daughter, Cami, does not perform all the exercises I've outlined in this course, but she does enjoy taking part in my workout schedule. As long as a stretching exercise is balanced with every exercise of contraction, there is no danger of binding a muscle or interfering with the natural growth process of a child. They can only benefit from progressive exercise. The hardest part is holding their attention for a sustained period of time. Children are indoctrinated by many misinformed adults that if a sport does not involve some form of contest or team effort, it is not worthwhile. So we balance our weight training with running over these Vermont hills, bicycling, hiking and, of course, skiing. In addition, Cami takes ballet classes, an opportunity no wise parent should deprive any little girl.

Fig. 1-10 (Above): *Angulation* at the completion of a turn, or when traversing, is at optimum balance when the torso is precisely perpendicular to the angle of the hill. This side bend utilizes the external oblique muscles at the waist.

Fig. 1-11 (Below left): SIDE BEND 1. **Extension** of the right external oblique muscle.

Fig. 1-12 (Below): SIDE BEND 2. **Contraction** of the right external oblique. Compare Cami's position here with Marge's angulated skiing position in Fig. 1-10.

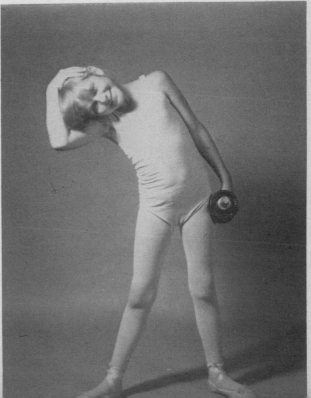

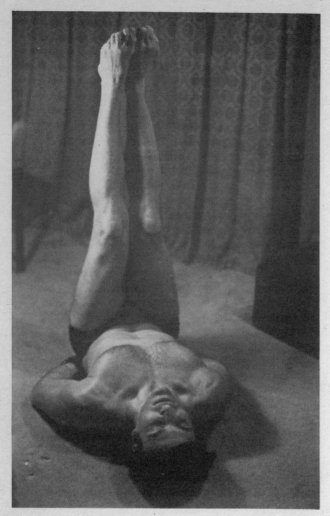

Fig. 1-13: LEG RAISES. Place your hands under your buttocks, raise legs perpendicular to the floor and slowly lower them to a point just above the floor, then return them to the vertical position.

Exercise 7: LEG RAISES (Fig. 1-13)

With no rest after Exercise 6, (you should be sweating by now, and your heart rate should be close to 75 percent of your maximum index), proceed to a clear area on the floor and take the position shown in Fig. 1-13. From this vertical position of your legs, lower them to a space about 6 inches off the floor, slowly. Without touching the floor, raise to the first position and continue. See how many reps you can squeeze out. My daughter's record is 72! If your performance is considerably less, you need this exercise, daily. Should you perform more than 25 in good form, strap on some ankle weights. You can pick up a pair at any good sports store. Do three sets of your maximum number of repetitions with active rest in between.

Exercise 8: SIT-UPS (Fig. 1-14)

Everyone seems to hate this exercise, and it's probably the one we all need most. Consider that the stomach muscles—the rectus abdominals which wall in the stomach—are used every time you turn a pair of skis and especially when that turn is made over a mogul. The abdominals run vertically from your sternum bone all the way to your pubic area. They are best exercised in a state of contraction. Hyperextension can stretch the abdominal muscles, and although they may strengthen, they will grow in size, creating a protuberance very easily mistaken for a pot-belly. Once stretched in this manner, only surgery can reduce the mass. For this reason, we should concentrate upon "crunching" the "abs" and holding the contraction for a count of three before stretching, and the stretch should not be extreme. The method I have found most effective is shown in Fig. 1-14. Hook up a strap to a bench to hold down your lower legs, or have a partner sit on them. Be sure to hold the contraction for a count of three, then lower the torso and continue for as many repetitions as you possibly can bear. Should you be strong enough to exceed 25 reps, hold a 10-pound plate behind your head for greater resistance. Three sets with active rest in between, then on to Exercise 9. You should be breathing pretty hard. Breathe in through your nose to filter unpurified air and exhale forcibly through your mouth.

Fig. 1-14: SIT-UPS. With legs on a bench is the best position for sit-ups. You will get maximum contraction with less repetitions necessary for optimum development.

Fig. 1-15 (Above): FLIES 1 (Extension). Stretch position for "flies," Note slight bend at elbows.

Fig. 1-16 (Right): FLIES 2 (Contraction). Tense your chest muscles when you return to this position of pectoral contraction.

Exercise 9: FLIES (Fig. 1-15 Fig. 1-16)

Some skiers might question the inclusion of upper body exercises in a program designed for skiing. If you think that our sport requires no muscular effort above the waist, talk to a few beginners about where they feel aches and pains after the first few days on skis. For that matter, speak to *any* skier who has spent a full day learning a difficult maneuver, and you will realize that skiing taxes *every* muscle. It is one of the most totally demanding sports and is thus one of the most totally conditioning sports that we know. Flies are the best exercise for development of the massive pectoral muscles which cover the chest. Aside from the pectorals' useful function in pole planting, in anticipation movements, and in assisting your rise from a fall, heavy development of the pectorals will give you a thick plate of muscular insulation against the cold, and, if you're a woman, a natural brassiere. Your clothes will drape better, too, instead of looking like they're hanging from a wire

hanger with no body beneath them. Take the position shown in Fig. 1-15 as you inhale. A slight bend at the elbow will put less stress upon it. Raise the dumbells to the position shown in Fig. 1-16 as you exhale, and repeat. Begin with light weights for a fast set of 25 repetitions to get the blood concentrated in the chest area. Follow with greater poundage and three *slow* muscle and strength developing sets; no more than 10 repetitions in these sets, and the tenth rep should be difficult! If it is not difficult, use more weight. Actively rest between sets for no more than 1 minute.

Exercise 10: INCLINE BENCH PRESSES (Fig. 1-17 and Fig. 1-18)

This exercise will move the blood concentration from the chest outward toward the shoulders and arms. Since it will develop the upper portion of the chest, just below the clavicle bones, it can serve to the advantage of men or women, par-

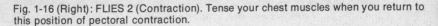

Fig. 1-17 (Left): INCLINE BENCH PRESSES 1. First position. Touch the bar to your chest for full extension of the pectoral muscles. We bought this weight guide from Weider Barbell Co. It's a very practical device if you work out alone.

Fig. 1-18 (Below): INCLINE BENCH PRESSES 2. Second Position. No need to lock out elbows while incline pressing. From this position, lower the weight *slowly*.

Fig. 1-19 (Left): UPRIGHT ROWING 1. Starting position. Keep your grip as shown, legs spread, chin up, chest out.

Fig. 1-20 (Above): UPRIGHT ROWING 2. Position of contraction. Hold it for a count of three, then lower the weight.

ticularly if it is performed without locking the elbows straight. Take the position shown in Fig. 1-17 (no warm-up is necessary, if you begin right after Exercise 9). Slowly push the barbell straight upward to the position shown in Fig. 1-18. Press no farther, but hold this position of contraction for a count of three, then lower for another rep. Do three sets of no more than 10 repetitions, but make that tenth one tough by using enough weight. Active rest for a minute, then on to Upright Rowing, Exercise 11.

Exercise 11: UPRIGHT ROWING (Fig. 1-19 and Fig 1-20)

To move the blood concentration directly into the deltoids—the muscles that cap your shoulders—Upright Rowing can't be beat. And, if you have ever had to rise from a fall on flat terrain, you'll believe that a skier needs shoulder muscles. Begin as shown in Fig. 1-19 with your back as flat as possible, chin up and shoulders tensed. Lift the barbell to the height shown in Fig. 1-20 and hold for a count of three before lowering to first position. One warm-up set of 20, then two heavy sets of 10 should be sufficient.

Exercise 12: LATERAL RAISES (Fig. 1-21 and Fig. 1-22)

Another shoulder exercise. This one really isolates the deltoids. Women should keep their repetitions high using a light weight for shoulder exercises to avoid building massive deltoids. Men can never get too big in this area, nor too

Fig. 1-21 (Below): LATERAL RAISES 1. Note slight tilt of torso for better deltoid concentration. This shows the point of greatest stress.

Fig. 1-22 (Right): LATERAL RAISES 2. Raise to an overhead position. Work alternate arms with no rest in between.

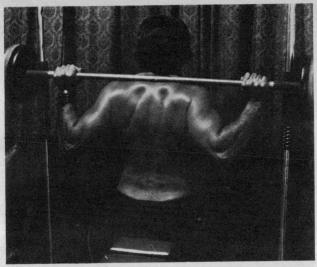

Fig. 1-23 (Above): PRESS BEHIND NECK 1: First position should be as low as you can manage for presses behind the neck.

Fig. 1-24 (Right): PRESS BEHIND NECK 2: Press only this far. Locking out can damage elbow joints.

strong, so keep your poundages high and perform no more than 10 repetitions after your warm-up. Warm up with a light weight and 25 repetitions. Alternate with each arm with no rest in between. One shoulder muscle will be resting while the other is working, and your cardiovascular system will benefit from this continuous exercise over the sustained period of your workout. First position is shown in Fig. 1-21. Then, slowly raise the dumbell to the position shown in Fig. 1-22. Peak contraction occurs when the arm is about parallel to the ground. Hold it there for a count of three before raising to the next rep. Lower the dumbell slowly for the added benefit of negative tension. Follow with a minute of active rest and move on to Exercise 13.

Exercise 13: PRESS BEHIND NECK (Fig. 1-23 and Fig. 1-24)

Call it male chauvinism if you will, but I think that this shoulder, trapezius, and triceps developer should be reserved for men. This exercise will thicken the entire shoulder and upper back girdle to give you natural shoulder pads. Great for softening the impact of falls while skiing, but not too attractive on women, if developed massively. Begin with a light warm-up set of 25. Then, three slow sets of 10 with maximum poundage, but only push the bar as far as Fig. 1-24, tense for a count of three and return the bar to behind your neck. Proceed immediately to Exercise 14 with no rest.

Exercise 14: LATS PULL DOWN (Fig. 1-25 and Fig. 1-26)

The complete Latin name for the major muscle involved in this exercise is the latissimus dorsi. These are the wing shaped muscles that stretch from your armpits to your waist, spanning the lower half of your back. For skiing, the "lats" would be most useful in rising from a fall or for climb-

Fig. 1-25: LATS PULL DOWN 1. Preparation. Full stretch for first position. Feel your scapula bones swivel outward stretching your latissimus dorsi.

Fig. 1-26: LATS PULL DOWN 2. Contraction. Be sure to hold position of contraction for a count of three before extending slowly to first position. This is my favorite weight resistance exercise.

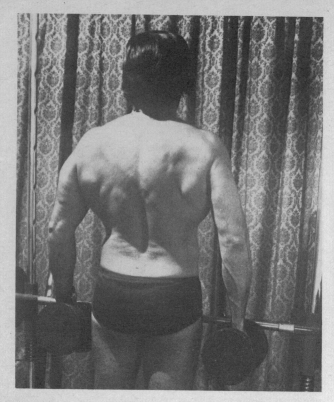

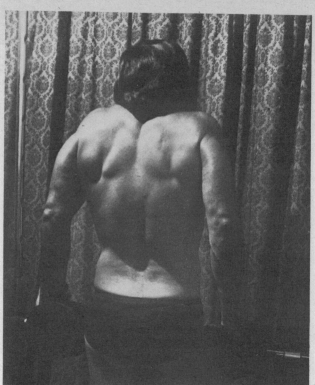

Fig. 1-27 (Above): SHRUGS 1. Many men and most women are very weak in the area of the upper back and neck. This exercise will strengthen the trapezius muscle and prevent the common "whiplash" injury that follows some falls. Begin as shown.

Fig. 1-28 (Above right): SHRUGS 2. Second position. Hold the peak contraction for a count of three, then lower to first position.

ing when you assist your steps uphill with pole plants. Light poundage and high reps for the girls; men can go heavy with less repetitions and more sets, for a massive V-shape. Begin as shown in Fig. 1-25 and pull slowly to the position shown in Fig. 1-26. Hold this latter position of contraction for a count of three and return the bar overhead, allowing a full stretch.

Fig. 1-29 (Below): FRENCH CURL 1. First position, which extends the triceps muscle on the back of your upper arm.

Fig. 1-30 (Right): FRENCH CURL 2. Triceps are contracted in this position. Don't lock the elbow, and keep the movement *slow*.

Three or four sets of no more than 10 reps, followed by a minute of active rest, then on to the "traps."

Exercise 15: SHRUGS (Fig. 1-27 and Fig 1-28)
To develop the kite shaped beautiful trapezius muscle which begins at the base of your skull, stretches to the shoulders and then dives toward the spine at an acute angle, try this exercise called Shrugs. Hold the bar as shown in Fig. 1-27. In Fig. 1-28 I am trying to touch my ears with my shoulders; this is the shrug. Tense for a count of three, before lowering your shoulders to the first position. Women should use a light weight to avoid bulking the traps excessively. Men use maximum poundage. Three sets of 10 reps with active rest in between.

Fig. 1-31: CURLS 1. Extension. Note slight bend at the elbow. This exercise really isolates the biceps muscle on the front of your upper arm.

Fig. 1-32: CURLS 2. Contraction. Here is where the maximum effort must be sustained. Hold the position for a count of three before lowering the weight.

Exercise 16: FRENCH CURL (Fig. 1-29 and Fig. 1-30)

No research by our office has turned up the reason why this exercise should be called French. It is a fantastic movement for triceps development, sadly neglected in both sexes as indicated by the flab that hangs below many adults' upper arms. While skiing, you use this muscle every time you plant a pole. Women should keep their reps high with a light weight for resistance. Men should use maximum poundage. Three sets of 10 after a warm-up set of 15 with a lighter weight. Take the position shown in Fig. 1-29, and raise the dumbell slowly to the height shown in Fig. 1-30, *without moving your elbow*. Work each arm alternately with no rest in between. One minute of active rest, then on to the last exercise. By this time, you have no doubt that you have been working!

Exercise 17: CURLS (Fig. 1-31 and Fig. 1-32)

Women who don't want a huge mogul on the inside of their upper arm may dispense with this exercise. Other exercises you have already performed have worked this muscle sufficiently. Most men don't mind the bump. For centuries, massive development of the biceps on men has been a symbol of great strength. Children are awed by a large flexed biceps, and it makes a great pillow for your wife's head. When we

ski, this muscle is called upon every time we rise from a fall, every time we climb, and every time we should be unfortunate enough to have to ride a rope tow. It also comes in handy for picking up fallen children and attractive snow-bunnies. There are many variations of the "curling" movement. The most effective that I have found begins extended as shown in Fig. 1-31. The dumbell is raised slowly to the position shown in Fig. 1-32. Do a fast set with a light weight to accelerate the heart rate and summon nourishing blood to the biceps area. Then, three sets of 10 with maximum poundage, alternating with each arm, and no rest in between.

Finish your workout with a relaxing swim or another set of Jumping Jacks. There are hundreds of other weight lifting exercises and developmental theories, but our intention here is not to build a nation of Arnold Schwarzeneggers or Raquel Welchs, we only wish to athletically condition your body for the mastery of the strenuous sport of skiing. Try the routine for 6 weeks. No one has to know that you have begun the program. Watch what happens in an incredibly short period of time. I have a hunch that training with weights may have a strong (no pun intended) affect on your whole life-style. More efficient skiing will be but one of your welcome rewards!

Chapter 2
EQUIPMENT TO CONSIDER

Skis—Selection and Care

AS IF IT WEREN'T enough that the ski industry should include two dozen different ski manufacturing brands, within each of those brands the skier is often confronted with another dozen choices in model designations and sizes. Perplexing. The wise tyro will *rent* his equipment for his first week's experience, as his learning process will be facilitated by the use of shorter skis. As the tyro's skill improves the ski length should be a graduated selection correlated to his or her progress and the grade of the slope he or she intends to challenge. The recreational stance for optimum balance when skiing with parallel skis straight down the fall line (the line of least resistance) seems to require a plumb line from the skier's throat through his arches—a straight line slightly more forward than perpendicular to the slant of the slope. Thus the skier's stance requires sufficient forward flex of the ankles to place the knees over the toes, and a slight bend at the waist. On a gentle grade a shorter ski is sufficient for balance and perhaps even preferred, as it will be easier to turn. On a steep slope, however, the perpendicular stance would feel awkward on short boards and insecure, particularly if the terrain is undulated or changeable in texture. On such terrain the short board skier would feel top heavy and about to do a forward somersault. Short board skiers compensate for this imbalance by sitting back and skiing on their tails—a dubious alternative method and certainly one that is less controlled. Part of your selection of ski length, then, is dependent upon how steep the slopes are that you normally ski. The other part has to do with your height.

What length ski should you begin with? There are so many opinions. Clif Taylor's "shortee" skis were not much longer than his boots, but the turns taught by Clif and his followers were skidded turns with the skis spinning flat to the snow surface. These skis had no "waist"—a side camber carved on the edges of more sophisticated skis designed for controlled turns. Some ski schools still teach beginners to turn on a "flat" ski, reserving edge control (transverse leverage) for a later lesson. It has been my experience to note that skiers who are taught to skid their turns early in their learning process have greater difficulty learning to carve on the skis' edges than students who learn to use their edges as early as their first day. My personal survey of student preferences and of successful ski lengths among learners seems to indicate that the ideal length for a beginner should be shoulder high. Any advice you might read specifying a certain length of ski for a beginner, for example "beginners should use 130cm skis," is absurd, as beginners come in many different heights. Inter-

mediate skiers might feel more comfortable on skis equal to their own height, while advanced recreational skiers would probably enjoy their sport on skis which climb to a point between their elbow and wrist, with their arm reaching overhead. Racers choose longer lengths because long skis travel faster and are more stable at higher speeds.

The flex pattern of a ski affects its performance considerably. Years ago, all skis were quite stiff. We had to jump our

Just a sample of all the various brands of equipment the skier has to choose from.

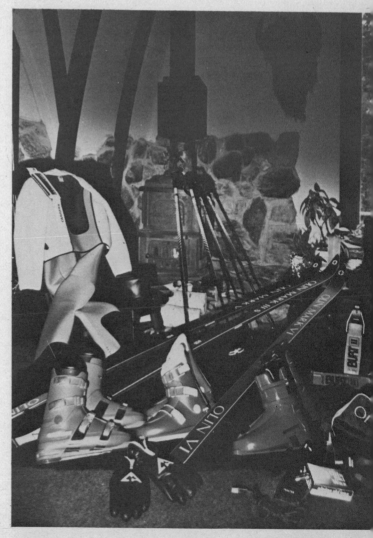

Fig. 2-1: Flex patterns can be examined in a cursory way by any recreational skier.

hold the shovel with one hand and with the other hand press different areas of the ski (Fig. 2-1). Some skis are softer at the tips than at their tails. Soft tipped skis with only a moderate sidecut or waist are designed for long carved GS turns (Giant Slalom turns) and for irregular terrain (the soft tips ease over the bumps). With a narrower waist, these same skis would be more appropriate for short radius turns or slalom, although the preference for stiff versus soft tips continues to be a running argument among slalom racers. Very soft tips do not hold well on ice, as they allow excessive tail slippage.

I believe that the best recreational ski for proficient skiers, who ski on snow less than a foot deep, is a ski which is softer at the shovel than at the tail, has a narrow slalom sidecut, a well curved tip splay, is light in weight and has edges made of hard enough steel to prevent filing every night. A ski with one continuous edge has extra spring, especially advantageous if you're interested in aerial maneuvers. Skis with "cracked edges" are purportedly better for snaking over the moguls, and for maintaining a constant continuous edge bite. This year, I am especially fond of my American-made Olin Mark Vs, which have all the characteristics of an excellent slalom ski plus a grooveless bottom for that saving skid, which we all feel is necessary to call upon occasionally (Fig. 2-2). For snow above the knees or wilderness variations, I would choose a shorter softer ski like the Olin Mark III-S, the Head Outback, or the Rossignol Salto. The extreme reverse camber that your body weight will bend in a soft ski makes turning easy in deep snow.

Fig 2-2: The grooveless Olin ski bottom. Will it begin a trend with this precedent?

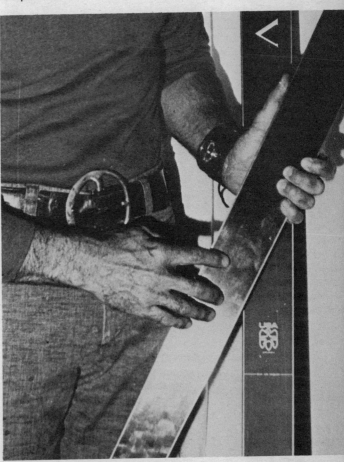

turns around, pivoting on our shovels (the front part of the skis). This is still an effective manner of descending a steep packed slope (see the *short swing* turn illustrated in Chapter 3). Most of today's recreational skis are more "forgiving." They are designed with a softer longitudinal flex which is great for powder and deep snow and exceptionally good for slow speed turns. Many of them are wide in the waist also, allowing for sloppy skidded turns which seem to satisfy the egos of many novice and intermediate skiers. This "wide waist" characteristic is what the industry refers to as a "forgiving" one in their bottom of the line recreational skis. Remember how popular the original Head Standards were? They were the pacesetters. Today, the straight boards are even softer and some even have a moderate waist. With sharp edges, skis which are considered "soft" will perform well even on packed snow. The only place they might give you trouble is on "boiler plate" or ice. To examine a ski's flex pattern, brace the tail of the ski against the inside of your foot,

Fig. 2-3 (Left): Soft skis like Olin Mark III-S bend easily into a reverse camber, allowing just a drive of my knees forward and uphill to carve a beautiful turn in soft snow.

Fig. 2-4 (Above): The Olin Ski Tuning Kit has all you need to keep your own skis performing well.

You have only to steer with your knees (Fig. 2-3).

I mentioned filing. In the East, it is almost a nightly ritual, as we are more likely to scrape over hidden stones than our more spoiled western neighbors. Some recreational skiers never introduce their skis to the file or to the waxing iron. Then they wonder why they can't perform as well as their instructors who wear out lots of files and burn pounds of wax in one season. For most purposes, your edges should be at the same flat level as your ski bottoms. (I read in a trade magazine that Bill Kidd likes to bevel his edges to rock from edge to edge quicker, but I question this practice when it comes to skiing ice.) A good flat filing should begin every season, as some P-Tex ski bottoms sink, while others might rise into convexity over the hot summer months. The former pro-clivity is a particular hazard called "railed edges." Such a ski will give you great difficulty turning, as it will want to track straight. Pick up a file. A good (excuse the expression) "mill bastard" file works best. Better yet, look into one of the many kits that are available. Inexpensive and superior is the one provided by Olin (Fig. 2-4) which includes all the equipment you need for filing or waxing. Your local ski shop will have it.

You will need a good brace to hold your ski while you are filing. After years of building and rebuilding brace devices every season, I finally solved the problem by springing for the pro-model Ski' Old Portable Vise—an ingenious device that is compact and efficient (Fig. 2-5). Easy to assemble, this apparatus comes with full instructions plus some excellent advice on ski maintenance. If you can't find one at your local

Fig. 2-5: The Ski' Old Portable Vise is a practical accessory for serious recreational skiers.

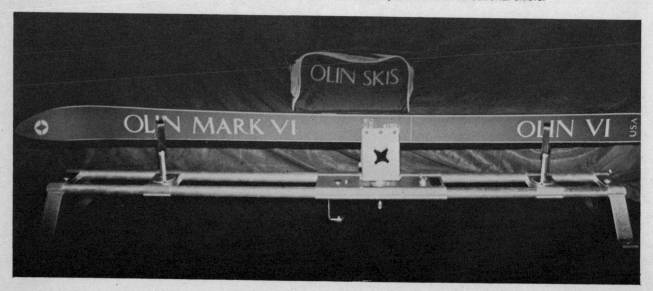

ski shop, write to Bek Products, P.O. Box 5047, Walnut Creek, California 94596.

Waxes make the skis glide better, prevent hesitation by reducing friction, and they prevent the nuisance of snow sticking to the bottom surface of your skis. Colors used to be standardized, and still are among the better brands: green for sub-zero; blue for most winter conditions; red for around freezing; and yellow for above freezing. (Write to U.S. Ski Wax, Box 4386, Denver, Colorado 80204, to find your closest dealer for their superior quality inexpensive ski wax.) There are now many variations and combinations of waxes, all designed to attack friction and of course to drain our pocketbooks. Though the different brands conflict in their color designations, each company fortunately supplies a leaflet describing the contents and their applicability.

Hot waxing is best. I prefer to drip it off a hot iron, then iron it. Most pros use this method, but be forewarned: Last season, during a hot waxing session, my iron was too hot. The

Metal to metal contact is the most reliable for release, and this simple fact has led most major binding manufacturers to include at least one plate binding in their line. It is more than coincidence that many rental shops in this country have converted their stock to include plate-type bindings, and the ski patrol officers I have interviewed have logged no fractures among skiers who have used plate bindings that were properly set for release! Burt remains the only binding that releases in every direction and is *retractable,* a unique feature which eliminates the necessity of a runaway strap (Fig. 2-6). Clipped by a minor avalanche while wilderness skiing a few years ago, one skier I interviewed can remember his Burts opening and snapping back several times as he rolled and was battered and spit out of the terrorizing current. He skied away from the slide without ever needing to adjust his bindings! What convinced the author of their worth was when I bird-dogged a well-known binding analyst whose name makes binding manufacturers tremble, as he is impeccably honest in his well

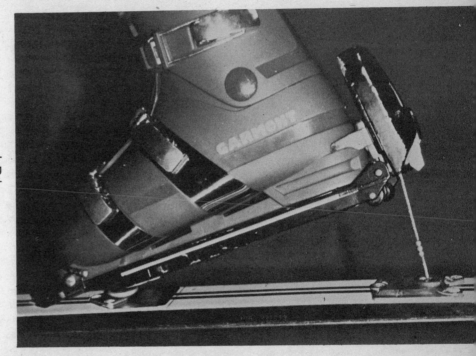

Fig. 2-6: The Burt release binding in action. In the event of a fall, the binding releases, the cable extends and then retracts! You never lose your ski.

wax sizzled on the base of my Head Slaloms and lifted the bottom lamination. Keep your iron low enough to just barely melt the wax. It shouldn't smoke. *Be sure to never keep the iron in one spot too long* or you might damage your best friends! The Olin Ski Tuning Kit includes a good iron and a variety of waxes. Ironed wax should be scraped and buffed to a thin, super smooth texture when the day is cold. When the temperature rises, the ironed wax should be left a bit irregular, as the thin covering of water which floats above the surface of melting snow will create suction between it and a smooth sliding ski. The best waxing technique for this latter condition is *brushing* of the wax in stepped, overlapping strokes from tail to shovel.

Bindings

I have often plugged the Burt as the safest most advanced design in ski bindings, and I've predicted that Burt's plate concept would revolutionize the industry. It is happening.

published appraisals. I wanted to see what *he* wears for his own recreational skiing. He's an incredible guy, who has taken some of the meanest eggbeater falls and tumultuous crashes in order to truly test all the products on the market. He could have as many sets of bindings from any manufacturer in the entire world—free. For his own skiing, he prefers Burts—for himself, and for his family.

In the past I have criticized the Burt's heavy weight plus the oversight of their not producing a children's model. My competition Burts are a bit heavy, but that would only be irritating to skiers who take a lot of air. The extra weight will not affect your ground skiing, except perhaps to improve it! My jumping levels were pared when I began to use the heavy Burt Comps. Since the jumps were never very high anyway, I barely got off the ground during my season on the retractable binding. Now, just when my legs have developed sufficiently from training with weights, extra altitude is no problem. But, wouldn't you know—Burt has come out with a new design, called the Burt

Fig. 2-7 (Right): The remarkable Burt II. Function and simplicity. A trend setter in the industry.

Fig. 2-8 (Below): Garmont racing boot for children snapped into the safest kids' binding made. The Burt Lite—a wise choice for the anxious parent!

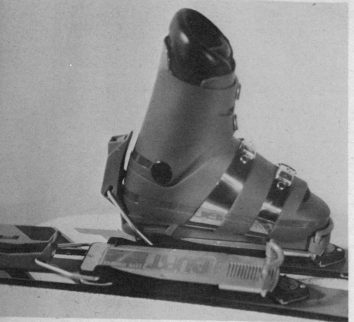

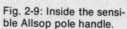

easily; they have *hollow, sharp edged points* for puncturing blue eastern "powder"; their handles are *contoured and molded;* and the material they are made of is *durable*. The molded and contoured handle is a questionable feature among veteran skiers, including the author, who feel inhibited by the close fit, as opposed to older strap-type models which allow a freer swing from the wrist and are easier to carry on the chairlift. Lacking straps, the contour handled poles are also a nuisance to climb back uphill after, when you've taken a mean fall and have slid 50 feet below the pole you lost. Their saber-like profile is handsome, though, and every one of the major manufacturers has adopted the molded pole handle design, so we must learn to live with it. For length, I prefer a pole that will stand as high as my armpit from the floor, when I'm standing in street shoes with low heels. For me, at 5 feet 8 inches, that amounts to a 48-inch ski pole. Some bump skiers prefer them shorter, but I find that a short pole makes you squat when you ski, and I prefer a taller stance.

This year, I have chosen the Allsop for myself and my family. It has all the fine qualities of top brand poles plus an added feature which is truly unique and considerate. The new feature is in the handle (Fig. 2-9). It is such a sensible idea, you may wonder, as I have, why no one ever thought of it before: A *spring* core to absorb the shock of that inadvertent

II, which is incredibly *light* and has but a single tension adjustment (Fig. 2-7). In addition, they are producing a Burt Lite retractable model for children who weigh less than 88 pounds (Fig. 2-8). Perhaps the most notable feature of the Burt, apart from its incomparable safety features, is that you can use the same binding on several pairs of skis, purchasing only the necessary small mounting plates for a nominal fee.

Poles

As confusing as the selection of skis might be, the number of poles on the market keeps up with the perplexing pace. Is one as good as another? What should you look for? What length? What kind of handle? What color? Again, I can only offer you my opinion, as your particular needs may differ from mine. Along with my opinion, though, I'll pass on the reasons which have formulated my choice.

Most top brand ski poles have similar characteristics in their top-of-the-line most expensive models. The best are cheap, so why not go for the best? They are *light,* to swing

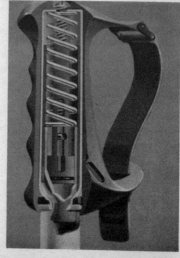

Fig. 2-9: Inside the sensible Allsop pole handle.

rebound, when we jam our pole into a formidable mogul! Now, we should know that pole plants are triggering deflections which were never taught to be forceful stabs, but who among the intrepid has not ripped through a bubbling mogul garden, teeth clenched, with piercing eyes and piston knees, and has not occasionally been more than gentle with the pole plant? A powerful deflection can tear the bursa at your shoulder joint. It has been known to rip ligaments, to strain the lateral deltoid or pull the triceps muscle. The spring in the Allsop handle is a special blessing to those of us whose age is around the half century mark; we don't heal as fast. Nordica thought the absorption concept was so sensible they put a spring in the heel of their ski boot for meeting the shock of flat landings from aerial maneuvers! Well, this author believes that the pole handle by Allsop makes a lot of sense, and it is probably only a matter of time before the patent is marketed to other consumer-need oriented pole companies. I congratulate Mike Allsop and his associates for another revolutionary idea which makes our sport all the more pleasurable and physically undamaging.

Ski Boots

Here we go again. Which one for you? What should you look for? How much should you spend? I can think of no time in the skiing experience when your knees should not be in a plumb line with the toes of your boots. Yes, even in *avalement*, when your knees are lifted to accommodate for the abrupt rise of ground level, leading the boots with your knees will ensure control of your ski tips when you stretch out on the other side of the bump. And yes, even in deep powder, when you might *think* that good skiers are sitting back, their knees are leading their boots in order to steer the skis. If your knees are leading your boots, your skis will go in any direction that you point your knees! That is your steering constant. That doesn't change in any skiing maneuver, except perhaps for an extreme "wheelie," where you pivot on your ski tails, but the wheelie performer had better be fast to recover after the pivot, and recovery means getting the knees ahead of the boots, or he will soon execute a back head plant! Well, if the knees in a plumb line with the boot toes is the optimum position, why not have the knees pressed forward by angling the boot shaft forward and raising the heel? Most top of the line boots have this built in *vorlage* which makes skiing a lot easier for advanced skiers than it is for beginners who have been advised to purchase a "beginner boot" for its comfort. Sure, its right angle makes walking more comfortable, and sure, it is certainly cheaper, but, in the long run, such a boot will make you work three times as hard as it is necessary to make a pair of skis perform.

If you have a budget problem, rent your skis and sleep in a cheap dorm, but don't hedge on the price of good boots. Buy the best, and make sure that they fit! The *best* boot is a warm one that fits properly, is comfortable and yet performs with precision. A *proper fit* and *comfort* are not necessarily redundant, since by proper, I mean fitted for function, and by comfort, I mean fitted for pleasure. The two are not synonymous. The boot should do more than keep your foot warm and give your ankle support. Your decision to apply leverage to your skis should be transmitted without hesitation; a good boot will assist your physical energy in achieving instantaneous response. The material from which it is made should be strong and durable. Leather outside shells are obso-

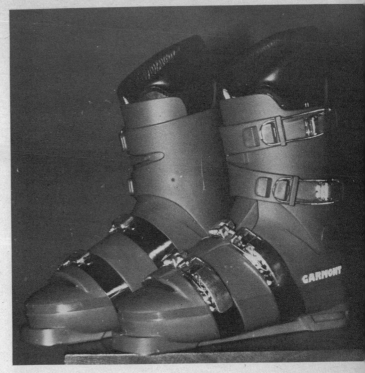

Fig. 2-10: The Garmont Gara is easy to spot in racing competition. Just look for the steel bands that wrap around it.

lete because they soften with age, and the primary function of a shell is to provide rigidity to the foot and ankle for transverse leverage. The inner boot is as important a consideration as the shell. Look for a footbed that has a built-in arch support and a snug heel cup. Couple that with a fat, shin loving cuff and boot tongue and you're looking at a quality boot.

This year, another American company, Garmont, has really joined the major league in supplying all of the good features I have mentioned plus an Airflex Fit System which is better than the more common *flow* material, to fill in the voids in front of and behind the ankle bones. The Airflex is light and highly insulative. New also, and unique to the Garmont racing boot, called Gara, is the banded shell concept which provides optimum closure and security without shell distortion (Fig. 2-10). These steel bands allow for maximum power and edging precision, combining a stiff rigid lower boot with a partially free, longitudinally hinging upper for shock absorption. Garmont's leather inner boots are less likely to cause skin irritations and more likely to wick moisture away from the feet. A dry foot is a warm foot. Garmont, first to produce plastic boots in Italy, may be a new name to some stateside skiers, but it is the number one selling boot in Canada and the second largest ski boot manufacturing company in the world! My first contact with Garmont was at the beginning of last season. I was in Vancouver to tape a season of weekly television "Chalk-Talks" on skiing with Ornulf Johnsen, ski school director of the Grouse Mountain ski school. Hours under the hot studio lights in full ski costumes made our feet swell with perspiration, and I can remember commenting to Ornulf how uncomfortable my feet were. He wiped the sweat from his large forehead and surprised me by saying that his feet were the only part of him that was comfortable. He was standing in Garmonts. I was in my favorite pair of quite stiff and relent-

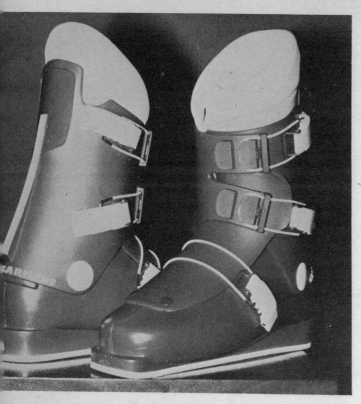

Fig. 2-11 (Above): Garmont's Omnilite provides light weight in a superior performance boot.

Fig. 2-12 (Below): Futuristic Diamond model hides the buckle. Another precedent by Garmont.

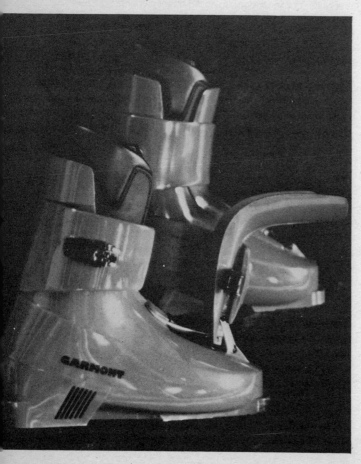

less racing boots. My curiosity was next aroused when Garmont moved their executive offices to our neighboring town. This gave us a chance to visit and closely appraise their products. Not without a chip on my shoulder, I might add, since I have been quite happy with my ski boots manufactured by another company for many years. The one characteristic of those old work horses that I do consider a problem, however, is that they lack a forward hinge. Calf soreness, shin bruises and fatigue are quite common after a day of boogying the bumps. They have never been totally comfortable, but I have always assumed that total comfort must be sacrificed in exchange for maximum performance. That assumption cost me a sixth toe, or outgrowth of the metatarsal bone beside my small toe. Of course, my old boots were designed for Olympic level racing, not recreation, and for that kind of performance, they are hard to beat.

Well, along comes Garmont with a legitimate promise of both—*performance and comfort!* Winning on all the major racing circuits, World Cup, Nor-Am, and World Pro, their polyurethane Gara model will be easy to spot in the 1980 Olympics, as it is the only boot wrapped with the two metal bands around the foot portion of the shell. The band around shell concept is purported to provide optimum edging without having to choke your instep by overbuckling. This torsional stiffness below is complemented by a free flexing upper shell and most comfortably padded inner boot. The Gara is Garmont's top-of-the-line model, designed for professionals and serious skiers.

Lighter is the key word in modern ski boots, and the beautifully styled *Omnilite II* by Garmont (Fig. 2-11) takes the lead among the lightest and most practical this year. It has a polyethylene shell, nylon cuff and shell cover, *molded* inner shell and a simplified three buckle system, which many boot companies are adopting this season. The Omnilite II is a recreational boot which performs well enough to have been worn by at least one winner on the World Cup circuit for downhill racing! It is for aggressive skiers with its extreme forward cuff angle. While I prefer the more formidable Gara for precise edging, I must admit that I appreciate the incredible light weight of the Omnilites. This will be a tough decision for advanced skiers—like choosing between a Porsche and a Corvette.

Revolutionary this year is another model by Garmont, called the Diamond (Fig. 2-12). It boasts a wraparound plastic closure system which completely conceals the one buckle that secures the shell. Here is elegance and performance in a three-piece shell outside plus their new molded shell inside. An interesting innovation is the split in the front and back of the cuff, which should make mogul skiing less shin bruising.

Of course, there are many other models in the Garmont line, but we don't want to turn this chapter into a commercial advertisement. The three boots we have selected are truly innovative, and we believe that their exclusive characteristics will set the pace in the industry. All good boot manufacturers try to offer a variety of models, not to confuse the consumer, but rather to offer something for the great variety of consumer needs. I know at least one female skier who buys boots to "match her outfit." The boot must fit, so try before you buy. Of course the store won't let you take them to the slope on speculation, but you certainly can walk around in a pair while you're in the ski shop, and remember that the boot's primary function is ski performance and walking comfort. Rock for-

Fig 2-13: The futuristic Carreras with exciting design by Porsche. Marge doubles their use as an earband!

ward in your natural skiing stance and tell the salesman about any pressure points or areas of discomfort. If possible, have him lock you into a demo pair of skis, so you can test the boot's edging efficiency by rocking your foot from side to side. Fit and function should come first. The boot's cosmetic features should be a last consideration. If you are lucky, the boot for you will come in a color that will match your outfit. We applaud boot manufacturers like Garmont which still maintain a basic black and white in their selection.

Goggles

You might think of them as non-essential. I didn't own a pair until I became an instructor. At first it was cosmetic motivation. I hated the pointed Moriarty hats that every recreational skier seemed to wear. They made me look like the European cartoon character, Punch. I decided that the hat didn't look so humorous if a yellow pair of goggles was strapped around it—it even looked a bit *macho*. One day, while I was riding the lift on a typically depresssing gray day in Vermont, I looked at the snow which was skied out and dirty and realized that we hadn't seen the sun in 35 days. Something made me slip the yellow goggles off the Moriarty and over my eyes. Revelation! The goggles made the day seem sunny and cheerful. Everything was touched with gold. I enjoyed that run more than any I had taken in over a month! Later, when our ski school director insisted that all instructors take part in Giant Slalom and slalom races, I realized that the goggles were protective against pole splinters, and they also kept the eyes from watering at high speeds. Still later, I was introduced to the excitement of off-trail skiing. Through the woods, with sharp naked pine branches daring you to turn closer, the goggles were imperative for eye protection. As they developed from a frivolity to an essential, I began to look for characteristics which made some goggles better than others. They should fit comfortably. They shouldn't fog easily or scratch. They should be yellow for the gray days and dark for the days which are sunny, particularly at high altitudes. Apart from that, they should be good looking. Why not? In our favor is the fact that all the goggle companies compete for the best of these attributes, and each year the consumer profits from this competition.

This year, the bouquet must go to Carrera and Porsche, who have teamed up to bring us the last word in style, comfort, function and practicality. *Kudos* to them also for not making their brand name as large as their unusually wide velcro fastened holding strap. Some skiers look like walking billboards for ski industry manufacturers. This is a clever advertising ploy that is popular today in many other industries. Consider the raised letters on automobile tires or the giant signatures on designer scarves that some women wear. And when did you last see a pair of skis which did not have the manufacturer's brand name splashed all-over it. Oh, well. It's a Madison Avenue world we live in, isn't it? Would you believe the Carrera goggles we are applauding in this report are flexible enough to slip into a parka pocket, covered by the retaining strap which is the same width as the lens? The modern designed Carreras also have a good ventilating system which will allow air in to prevent fog and yet keep the snow out (Fig. 2-13). They come in black or white trim. Marge says that my black ones make me look like a bandit, while I think that her white ones make her look like a vision from outer space! A bonus is that the extra width of the strap functions as an additional ear cover on those bitter cold days!

Skins

From the moment you succeed at your first perfect turn, your involvement in skiing becomes a glorious up and down ego trip. The second day on skis you are already better than someone, and, since your first day was probably the most humiliating of your entire life, you will take secret pride in watching the struggle of the beginners who have yet to attain even your level of status in the skiing community. Then, it never stops. If you're wise, you look at those who lag behind your state of progress and work hard to stay ahead. The more foolish look upward at the performers—the experts—and the goal seems too distant, the impression is too overwhelming, the ego is butchered and the question becomes not "what can

Fig. 2-14: Freedom, warmth and classic styling characterize these "Gopher" outfits by Fitz-Wright.

I do to improve . . . ," but rather "what can I do to get out of this foolish commitment . . . ."

With each successful maneuver or conquest of a new challenging slope, a new self-assessment will probably take place. One thing you may reconsider is what you are wearing. If your skiing is done at a place like Mad River Glen, you look all over Canal Street for the right Army fatigue jacket (well-worn) and a pair of bleached out bib jeans—the uniform of the hotshots who boogie down the bumps. You may disregard the fact that the jeans will soak clean through when you fall, and you'll literally freeze your derrière off. If you do your thing at Sugarbush, it may be Saks Fifth Avenue and furs for you. If creativity is not your thing, you'll settle for the Moriarty hat, parka and stretch pants and get lost in the crowd. If you're a loner, you might rebel against conformity—you might wear a cowboy hat one day or just an Apache scarf around your forehead. One week you might opt for wolf and the next you might be stretched in neoprene. Skiing is a very individual sport, and the image that you create might be a truly unique one, or it might be quiet and conservative. At any rate, your skins will probably reflect your personality. Hopefully, your respect for practicality and comfort will transcend your egotistic motivation. Then, the outfit that you select will be *sufficiently warm* and will allow for *freedom of movement*. Its aerodynamic style might even show off your body, with the provision that you have a body that you are proud to show off. The choices are myriad and are limited only by the contents of your bankbook. If you want the best outfit to satisfy every practical and frivolous need, consider *neoprene*, and, if you're looking for the best of the neoprene skins, consider the "Gophers" (Fig. 2-14) by Fitz-Wright Manufacturing, Ltd., 17919 Roan Place, Surrey, British Columbia, V3S 5K1.

Neoprene is the stuff used for making "wet suits" used by skin divers and surfers. They are the warmest, tightest clinging stretch outfits you can buy, but, as with all other equipment, there are good and bad neoprene outfits. Some neoprene suits attract snow like a magnet. It clings to the material and makes it very difficult to hide the fact that you have fallen. The Gopher Skiwear by Fitz-Wright is unique, as its neoprene is thin and is laminated with nylon on the inside and lycra on the outside. The nylon inside lining makes the outfit a lot easier to get into and out of, but what makes the Gophers number one in our book is their classic formfitting design. A work of art in variations of blue and gray from the sketchbook of Gabriel Levy. Neat! Each suit is hand tailored to your own specific body measurements. If you are a camp follower, forget it. You'll be seen and admired in these skins. If you're proud of your bod and the skiing that you do, go for the Gophers. They are the closest thing to naked and free, and the warmest ski apparel you can find.

Writing a chapter on equipment for a book on such a progressive sport as skiing is a tough assignment. Almost as soon as my words have been published, manufacturers will be unloading their new line. Another problem is with regard to advertising. Obviously, all the top brand companies have excellent products to offer. We can't list them all in these limited pages, nor do we want our book to follow the precedent established by the trade magazines, which allow a volume of advertising to bury a few informative articles. For this reason, I have reported on my personal choices of new items to consider. Just as beauty is indeed in the eyes of the beholder, so skiing performance needs are totally subjective.

Chapter 3

SKI INSTRUCTION: The Parallel Method

IT IS POSSIBLE to teach yourself to ski, and it is certainly possible to learn how to ski without ever having to point one ski across the path of the other (the traditional "wedge" approach which is taught in most ski schools). The parallel approach to your learning process is safer, more practical, and certainly more graceful than the wedge or snowplow

Frank Covino and his wife Marge make turning on skis look easy — and it can be! Just follow the no frills skiing instructions in this chapter.

technique. The early stages of your skiing experience require no special athletic skill. You will, of course, learn a lot faster and with less physical pain (perhaps none) if you begin with a well tuned body, but we have just taken care of that in Chapter 1. You will also need a mind—I'm convinced that skiing is a head sport before being a physical one. With an understanding of the mechanics of gravity, forward and transverse leverage, and balance, in opposition to the resultant forces, called centrifugal and centripetal, any skier who is reasonably intelligent, alert and courageous can master the sport in one season, if he uses well designed and fine tuned equipment. That's a pretty heavy statement, but I can back it up with hundreds of success stories about skiers who I have trained. I'm happy to add that my record of over 8,000 lessons is marred by only one unfortunate accident. That broken leg was also the most shapely, as it belonged to my dear friend Doris Jansson, a Ford model who met her demise after ski class when one of her ski tips slid beneath the other as she flew down The Lord's Prayer run at Big Bromley, totally out of control. Her binding was rather primitive and did not release. Her technique was called the "snowplow." It was 1960. Rented equipment was poorly maintained and decidedly unsafe, and most rental boots were of soft leather with curled up toes. That incident marked the moment when I decided to question the traditional snowplow approach to ski learning. I really liked that leg of Doris', and it hurt to see it casted—and imagine her pain. Organized ski instruction at that time was not far behind where it is today at many ski areas. There must be another way, I thought, and I began to search the physics involved in the simplified turning of a pair of descending skis. My investigations led to the following basic conclusions:

1. The skis are sliding down the hill. You are merely a passenger. Body movements therefore are secondary.

2. The primary force behind the movement of descent is *gravity*, which will pull any weighted object that is not opposed by a blocking mass. The speed of that descent is dependent upon the amount of friction that is present to impede the velocity.

a. Skis that are flat to the snow surface will slide downhill, no matter which way they are pointed; snow, piled before the sliding skis can be of sufficient opposing mass to terminate the slide.

b. Flattened skis pointed across the slope (the traverse direction) and weighted aft will slide downhill tails first; centrally weighted, they will slip downhill sideways (called a sideslip); weighted at the shovels or ski tips, the splayed or curved front portion of the skis will lead the slip of the flattened skis downhill.

c. A sudden tilt of flattened sideslipping skis onto their uphill edges increases the friction beneath the skis and will stop the slide, as snow forms a blocking mass sufficient to oppose the gravitational pull. Such a tilt is called "transverse leverage."

3. Tilting or edging of the skis by transverse leverage is accomplished by angling the lower body (hips and knees) uphill. To maintain balance, the upper body must counterpoint by angling downhill. In a traverse direction, the precise angle for optimum balance is when the torso is perpendicular to the slant of the ground on which the skier stands, marked by the shoulders being parallel to the slant of the hill.

4. Flattened skis pointed downhill will descend tips first if the bodyweight of the skier is directed towards those tips. The skis may then easily be steered across the "fall line" (the line of the least resistance) by the inside hip and knees, but only if the knees are leading the ski boots during the steering action.

a. A movement of the knees and hip inside the turn will tilt the skis onto their inside edges. This transverse leverage will provide resistance against centrifugal force (the force that pulls away from the center of the turn). If the knees are leading the ski boots, pressure is created toward the inside edges of the ski shovels. This section of the ski is splayed (curved upward) and is usually wider than the waist or the tail of the skis. As the wider shovels dig into the snow on their inside edges they "spoon out" the arc of the turn, assisted by the side camber or waist of a well designed ski.

b. Balance is maintained by keeping the torso perpendicular to the slant of the slope, in opposition to the pull of centripetal force. This "angulation" will result in more bodyweight pressed against the inside edge of the outside ski, which becomes the downhill ski at the turn's completion.

c. Shovel pressure may be augmented by keeping the hands well forward when skiing straight downhill. The hands' position directly affects longitudinal leverage: In line with the ski tips, the pressure is forward, toward the ski tips; when the hands are carried at the sides, the pressure is over the center of the skis; carried behind the body, the pressure is aft.

6. As the pole plant marks the center of a short radius turn, it is best planted downhill (in the fall line). Thus, skiing straight downhill, the pole is planted close to the outside ski tip, as the shovels roll away from the fall line. When skiing across the hill (traversing), the pole is best planted to the side (downhill).

a. If the pole point is frozen 6 inches above the snow and planted by a drop of the knees forward and uphill, the camber of the skis is pressed flat against a resultant platform of snow created by the sudden transverse leverage.

b. This facilitates the next action, a spring of the skier's body upward, forward and downhill. This rapid forward leverage coupled with a flattening of the skis in a slow turn, or a roll onto the downhill (inside) edges in a fast turn, will be followed by a slip of the ski tips into the fall line and the inception of a turn. The force behind that slip is gravitational. The ski tips will move downhill first because they are, at that moment, the most heavily weighted portion of the skis.

I hope that jargon didn't overwhelm you before we even start. These were merely my first thoughts, 19 years ago, a radical departure from the traditional Arlberg system, but, I still feel, an accurate analysis. I have been forced to teach it underground, in order to maintain teaching positions under Ski School Directors who are more reactionary. My first book, *Skiing Made Easy* (NY Lancer Books, 1971) reluctantly conformed to the traditional snowplow, stem,

Classic angulation of Stein Eriksen compared to dribbling style of champion basketball player De Busschere proves there is nothing "unnatural" about the stance. If you were to walk across a steep hill in street shoes you would *naturally* drop your downhill shoulder, as your hip would angle into the hill and your uphill shoulder and hip would probably lead your stroll. The current depreciation of this form by P.S.I.A. methodology conflicts with the opinion of the author. Supporting Frank Covino are the thoughts of Othmar Schneider, Emo Henrich, Stein and other Ski School Directors.

stem christie, christie pattern. It had to—I was employed by a dogmatic Ski School Director who eventually gave me the axe, anyway. With the second edition of *Skiers Digest*, I publicly challenged the antiquated system and was blackballed by some of my PSIA colleagues for my radical efforts. Courage to spread the gospel of my convictions was helped by the innovative movement of other radical pros like Karl Pfeiffer, who inaugurated the sensible GLM (Graduated Length Method), a strictly parallel approach. Since then, many ski schools have awakened to deprecate the dangerous and awkward snowplow or wedge posture. As a result serious leg accidents have significantly declined. The parallel system works. Try it. The method is presented here for you to test. No frills. Your comments, pro or con, will be appreciated.

NO FRILLS SKI INSTRUCTION

FOR YEARS, the Ski School curriculum has been based upon the supposition that the learner is a kinetic idiot who skis once or twice a year for reasons other than the pure enjoyment of the sport. The effort in most schools still is to get that clown to turn as quickly as possible, so he can boast of his achievement back at the office and wait another year for his next lesson. So they teach him to spin. On the flat part of his skis. Like a propeller. He turns. He is happy. He will return. Next year. Granted, I have taught many of these day trippers, and I have taught the fat, the tall, the lean and the small, and maybe some of them were kinetic imbeciles. But a lot of them were not. A lot of them had good balance, an alert mind and were in excellent physical condition. It is to such learners that this chapter is dedicated. To the physically fit and the mentally aware, who should be taught differently than their less-capable cousins.

A ski instructor's training should include at least a basic course in psychology. Every student he teaches is as different and as individual as snowflakes. Their only common denominator is that they are in class to learn. They are uninformed. The uninformed ego is a complex phenomenon. At birth it screams for perpetual comfort, satisfaction of its basic needs, love and attention. After several years of frustration of having to *earn* these favors, it can either become incorrigibly extroverted, acceptably cooperative or passively withdrawn. The ostentatious are difficult to teach because they feel they "know it all" and are *above* needing instruction. The introverts are not easily taught because they doubt their capacity for success in any endeavor. The middle group usually welcomes instruction and learns with little effort because they have less "hangups" or personal inhibitions. Although they too may be unaware if their capacities, they at least welcome stimulus that tests their potentials. This chapter is directed at all three groups; toward the introverts and extroverts who have their peculiar reasons for not taking ski lessons from qualified ski instructors, and toward those skiers of the middle group who are open to direction but who may be disappointed with the instruction they have received on the hill.

The reasons for such disappointment can be many and varied. Here are some of the comments I have heard from some disgruntled students:

"The class was too big . . ."

"The students were not all at the same level . . ."

"He (the instructor) gave all his attention to the girls . . ."

"All our instructor did was show-off . . ."

"He talked too much . . ."

"He talked too *little* . . ."

"He took us on a slope that was too difficult . . ."

"He didn't teach the same system that I learned at Paradise Peak . . ."

"I couldn't understand his accent . . ."

The list of gripes is endless, and, as difficult as it may be for a student to adjust to a typical ski class situation, it is even more of a problem for an instructor. Consider these barriers to a successful *teaching* experience:

It's the Christmas-New Year's week and the penurious corporation has sold an excess of ski lesson tickets. You have a class of 15 students! (Eight should be maximum.)

Your incompetent ski school director has neglected to separate the groups of students according to their specific level of proficiency. You have five who are ready for parallel turns, six who have never been off a beginner slope, and four who are skiing against their better judgement (to please a husband, wife or child) and are wishing they had never come.

Three students are using antiquated equipment, or skis that are too long, or mixed brand binding combinations that are unsafe. Five students haven't had their skis waxed; the snow is caking to the middle of their ski bottoms and is preventing them from moving.

Two students, whose waists are bigger than the girth of their shoulders, can't get up by themselves when they fall. While you help them rise, the class is grumbling.

Four students haven't spent a winter day outdoors in 20 years. They are red-nosed and white-faced, trembling at an ideal 28 degrees, and impatient for the class to end.

You have just glided off the chairlift unloading platform, and there stands your class, in line. Two obese specimens are eating salami sandwiches, dressed in Army fatigues with their socks outside their pants. Two recalcitrant teenagers who shared a "joint" on the chairlift ahead of you are long haired and psychedelic in their discordant colored jumpsuits replete with racing stripes. Two gray-haired women want to rape you. Two drunks are man and wife and are arguing between themselves already. Two have frost-bitten ears. Two hate your guts because of your glamorous image. Your job? Keep them all happy for two hours and *teach*.

As you can see, an instructor's list of obstacles is also endless. Add to it the facts that he probably works a 7-day week, 6 hours a day, for less than the "minimum wage," frequently in sub-zero temperatures, rain or sleet, hardly has the time between lessons to relieve his kidneys and seldom has lunch, because the only way he can earn a few extra dollars is to teach on his lunch hour, and you have a very *un*glamorous picture of the ski instructor who tries so valiantly to deliver his lesson at a level of understanding that is effective to all.

There are many pros and cons when one considers the effectiveness of a ski class lesson. The question inevitably arises: can you teach *yourself* how to ski? My opinion, based upon 15 years of teaching experience, is that the art of skiing has a *scientific* basis. Anything scientific is logical and can be taught to any reasonably intelligent mind. Few of us have the mental discipline to learn anything by reading alone, however. Vicarious learning will never replace pragmatic understanding. Thorough knowledge must be the result of exposure to salient principles that you believe will help you to achieve success, plus empirical verification of those principles by extensive practice under the critical eye of a qualified professional. That kind of cumulative awareness is possible in the sport of skiing. There are enough publications available which reveal the science of skiing, and there are a sufficient number of instructors around who are qualified to judge and accelerate your proficiency at the practice of those principles.

Errors made by many technical manuals are that they either take too much for granted from the average reader, are too verbose or pedantic for basic understanding, are chauvinistic, or simply are too drawn out and lengthy for rapid understanding. In this chapter, I will try to avoid each of those barriers to your learning experience. The system that I will present is one that I have devised which is designed to help you master the art of pure parallel skiing in the shortest amount of time possible. It is qualified by my extensive experience in teaching the Modified Austrian Technique, the American Technique and the Stein Eriksen Ski School Technique, plus by my own training as a student under the tutelage of qualified French, Austrian, American and Canadian ski instructors. It is therefore an eclectic system which should simplify your whole learning process if you have the desire to teach yourself.

The Professional Ski Instructors of America has paved the way for a universal mastery of the sport by also borrowing the best theory from each of the international systems and simplifying your understanding. The basic differences between its ATM program and my pure parallel approach are as follows:

1—My Graduated Length Method, a personal adaptation of the original systems inaugurated by Clif Taylor and Karl Pfeiffer, encourages parallel movements *exclusively* while the P.S.I.A. continues the traditional approach of wedge-type exercises which I believe are invaluable to non-athletic skiers or those who are physically inadequate, but which are unnecessary, and in some cases detrimental, to the progress of the new skier who has little difficulty with other athletic or kinesthetic movements.

2—The student of the American Teaching Method and the almost identical method taught by the Canadian Ski Instructor Alliance is encouraged to employ skidding movements on the flat part of his ski in the early part of his learning process. I personally believe that the skill of positive edging should be taught to physically capable tyros on the very first day and employed as a discipline in every learning exercise.

3—Little mention is made in the ATM or C.S.I.A. program of body angulation. I believe that this classic position is so essential for controlled descents on steep or icy terrain that it should be taught early as a discipline and be consistently employed in each of the subsequent learning exercises when the skier is in a traverse attitude i.e., as the hip and knees are pressed to the uphill side of the skis for traverse leverage, the shoulders are angled to the same slant as the slope for balance. I am not alone in my defense of this form. Othmar Schneider, Olympic champion and Director of Skiing at Boyne, is vehemently opposed to the modern ski school's lack of emphasis upon this vital defense against the pull of centrifugal *and* centripetal force. Angulation is not a chauvinistic affectation. It is an imperative silhouette for optimum control and balance in most recreational skiing.

4—While other systems encourage a wide track approach for *all* beginners, (and I believe that such an approach may be necessary for the non-athletic or physically handicapped), I feel that many new skiers are as capable of learning to ski with their boots together as children are of mastering the skill of riding a bicycle without training wheels. There is no question in my mind about the "stability" of an open stance. I simply maintain that, if a student feels as stable with his feet together, he should not be discouraged from using this closed stance, as he will then add to the security of his stability the aesthetic quality of *grace*.

The current P.S.I.A. Technical Committee has adopted the mature attitude of flexibility within their teaching program. Their rejection of rigid final forms as stepping stones in the progress of every new skier is a refreshing attitude accepted by most other modern schools, bringing us closer to a universal method for teaching the art of skiing. It is hoped that my pure parallel approach, designed for the physically conditioned, alert new skier, will be accepted as part of that ubiquitous eclectic curriculum. Practice the following proposed exercises under the critical guidance of a qualified ski instructor, supplement a minimum of one week's on-the-mountain-instruction per season with at least ten private lessons from an eclectic minded ski instructor, and you will be skiing the expert slopes by next Easter!

A. PREPARATION

1. Some GLM Schools advocate 3-foot skis for the beginner. While such a ski does facilitate turning by axial motion, it also presents longitudinal leverage problems, particularly for the tall learner. I believe that the length of your first ski should relate to your height. Choose a pair of skis that are as high as your armpits (Fig. 3-2), preferably with *plate* bindings (they are safer); rent them, as you will need a longer ski in a few days (the Graduated Length Method). If you can't find a rental pair of skis with plate bindings, just make sure that the bindings which are attached to the skis that you rent are tested with a Lipe release check *while you are locked into them*.

2. Don't let any salesman con you into buying cheap beginner boots. If you are committed to learning this sport rapidly, the only boot for you is an expensive *expert* boot that fits well and will last for many years. It should have a high back to keep you from sitting back too far and raised heels to keep your knees in a plumb line with your toes, where they should be for optimum control. (Fig. 3-3) Your boots are your first and most important investment. A

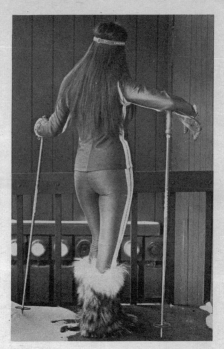

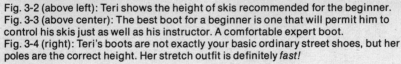
Fig. 3-2 (above left): Teri shows the height of skis recommended for the beginner.
Fig. 3-3 (above center): The best boot for a beginner is one that will permit him to control his skis just as well as his instructor. A comfortable expert boot.
Fig. 3-4 (right): Teri's boots are not exactly your basic ordinary street shoes, but her poles are the correct height. Her stretch outfit is definitely *fast!*

variable would be the Free Style type boot for those of you who would eventually move into that new phase of skiing. They have a slightly lower back and flexible hinge of the upper shaft to accommodate for miscalculated landings from aerial stunts and for fast, tight mogul busting.

3. Dress adequately, and pick a sunny day for beginning. You will have enough problems without worrying about severe cold and poor visibility.

4. Select poles that tuck just beneath your armpit when you are standing on the floor in ordinary street shoes (Fig. 3-4).

5. DON'T RIDE THE LIFT. Not yet. If you can't tolerate climbing a slight grade between each exercise on the first morning, you are not physically ready for skiing.

6. The skyrocketing import census for the state of Florida indicates that most of us find the severe cold of winter a needless ordeal. Who among even skiers would not settle for a season of just *spring* skiing? As I write at this moment, the thermometer outside our Vermont home shivers at 30 *below* zero. My car has three umbilical cords running from it to the house's electrical outlet: a motor block heater, an oil dip-stick heater, and a charger on the battery which was choked with ice. My right toe is burning from a touch of frostbite, and I have a dimple under my cheekbone from tissue destroyed by frostbite several years ago. Few sensible skiers ski when the thermometer dives below zero, but there will always be fanatics like Marge and myself who *have* to be out there when the slopes are white. For us, precautions *must* be taken. Here are a few tips which we have found helpful:

a. Don't overdress and stay that way when you are not outside. Even a short drive from your lodge to the ski area can make you perspire, and perspiration can freeze when you step outside that heat choked automobile. If you must drive to the area fully ski clothed, open the car windows; especially if there is a smoker in the car!

b. A dry anti-perspirant sprayed between your toes will prevent freeze-potential perspiration from accumulating there (I forgot, this morning . . .).

c. When the temp is sub-zero, a face mask is advisable if you haven't eased your face tolerance into the bite of winter winds. (They are not only made for bank robbers.)

d. Furs beat *any* kind of parka for warmth at sub-zero, hands down. Pick one from an unendangered species to appease the ecology freaks (Fig. 3-5).

e. Your head is your battery. Keep it warm and it will spark your reflexes. The Moriarty hats are adequate (for most of the season) but are not as effective in sub-zero temperatures as fur or cowboy hats (with ear flaps) which allow for air insulation. Brimmed hats also are great when it snows or rains, functioning as umbrellas. The ski school at Steamboat Springs uses cowboy hats as part of its uniform. Smart. I am surprised that more skiers don't use them.

f. A set of thermals under ballet tights is a great second skin for good insulation on the sub-zero days. The tights will help your feet to slip into your boots easier too. Fishnet shirts are recommended as the best underwear to have close to your skin; air pockets are the best insulation (Fig. 3-6).

g. A cup of hot soup in the lodge while you massage your toes will make the last runs of that sub-zero day much more enjoyable; massage hers, too . . .

h. Comfort Products, Box 9200, Aspen, Colorado 81611, has come to the aid of many skiers who have poor circulation in their extremities. Those funny looking boxes you may have seen on the back of some skiers boots are the power packs of their Footwarmer product, an electrical heating device that really works. Insoles of emboss-grained vinyl enclose a heating element that is a completely flexible etched foil circuit focused upwards toward the foot. The completely sealed power packs weigh about 15 ounces apiece and contain 4-volt systems with no shock or shorting hazard. Daily use does not affect the cycle life. They accept a full charge over a ½-hour period, with no overcharge danger. They are especially recommended for ski instructors, patrolmen and for any skier who spends more than a few hours

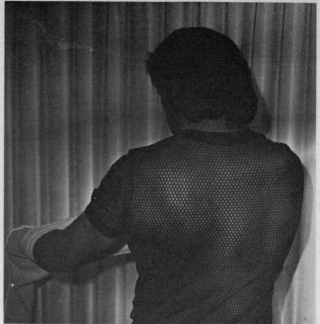

Fig. 3-5 (left): My wife says I look like *the bad guy* in an Italian western, but this is my warmest outfit on those sub-zero days. Marge sewed ear flaps onto the hat.

Fig. 3-6 (above): Best insulation you can have next to your skin is the *fish-net* type shirt.

in sub-zero or sub-tolerable temperatures. New from Comfort Products also is the world's first *electronic glove*, called the Lunar. I salute this United States company for solving the most common problems of skiing comfort. We hope that their contribution will bring back many skiing deserters who fled south with frostbitten fingers and toes, and we wonder: can an electronic *hat* be far behind? (Fig. 3-7)

7. More ski accidents occur after 3 PM than at any other time of day. This is due partly to the fatigue of skiers who are in poor physical condition, partly because of icier conditions than when the sun is high, and partly because of *poor visibility*. When the sun drops, its rays no longer expose undulating terrain and cause definitive shadows. You will then experience what is called *flat light*; the terrain looks flat and deceptively easy. Yellow goggles will not only help to define the slope variations; their golden glaze will actually have a psychologically beneficial effect in warming up the bleakness of overcast or sunless conditions.

While the sun *does* shine, do your eyes a favor and protect them with darker lenses, or you will soon sport that characteristic slash of red across the whites of your eyes that is so common among foolish skiers. The higher the elevation, the darker your lenses should be.

I can speak from personal experience to skiers who wear contact lenses. It is true that they do protect your pupils and are even better than goggles when it is snowing, as they won't fog. Colored lenses offer some brightness reduction; resistance to the ultra-violet rays of the sun is provided by special lenses which have been designed with this protection in mind. Available from Sight Improvement Center, Inc., 25 West 43rd Street, New York, N.Y. is a process called Ultra-Violet Inhibitor, which guarantees elimination of ultra-

violet rays from outdoor sun and even flourescent lights. The same company offers a WETreat (TM) adjustment to any contact lens, which improves optical clarity while allowing skiers to wear their lenses for a longer time; the treatment keeps lenses more moist for greater wearing comfort. My wife and I have been using UVI lenses with the WETreat adjustment with remarkable results, particularly at higher elevations.

Overexposure of your eyes to strong sunlight on the ski slopes during the day can result in poor vision after sunset, whether or not you wear glasses. Bright sunlight can destroy the normal quantity of "visual purple" in the eyes temporarily, and several hours are required to renew that supply. This accounts for reports from skiers about the "night blindness" that they experience when driving home after a ski weekend. It can be avoided simply by protecting your eyes with correctly tinted lenses or goggles when skiing in bright sunlight. Advisable colors are dark green, brown or gray tints; least acceptable for screening out harmful sun rays are yellow or blue lenses, according to the New York State Optometric Association. While yellow-lensed goggles are the ones most preferred by racers, they should really only be used on overcast days or in flat light. Most goggles are sold with interchangeable lenses for this reason. (Fig. 3-8)

B. SOME BASIC SCIENCE

1. **The Skier.** Basic science that will help your mastery of this sport should include a psychological analysis of you, the skier—skiing, I'm convinced, is a head sport. At this point, let's just say that each of us has a personal motivation for taking part in skiing, and no amount of exposure to technical principles can effectively teach any individual who has a

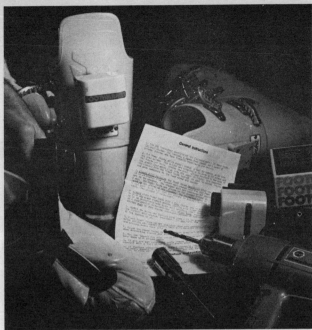

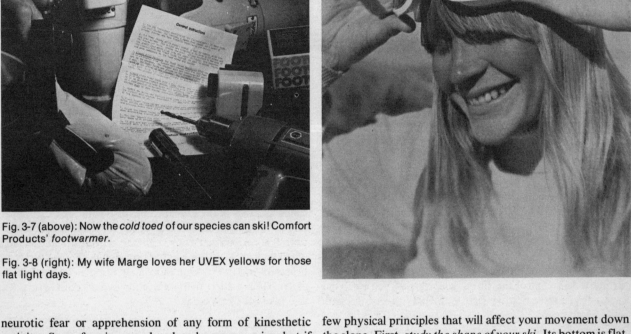

Fig. 3-7 (above): Now the *cold toed* of our species can ski! Comfort Products' *footwarmer*.

Fig. 3-8 (right): My wife Marge loves her UVEX yellows for those flat light days.

neurotic fear or apprehension of any form of kinesthetic activity. Some fear is normal and perhaps even wise, but if that emotion boils into a disproportionate form of horror, that person is asking for trouble, as skiing is an intellectual sport that demands exceptional self-discipline and control of one's mental and emotional faculties during every moment of descent.

What proved to me that *fear* is the primary deterrent to a skier's progress was the experience I had with David, a 24-year-old musician from Boston who was congenitally blind. My first thought, as I am sure you must have, is that nothing could be more fearful than not being able to see, but it was not long before I realized that David was at an *advantage*! He could not *see* the steepness of the slope; he could not *see* the ice patches; he could not *see* the uncontrolled skiers schussing before him; he could not *see* the lack of sun on that dreary overcast day. David's blindness blocked every stimulus for fear and apprehension that the rest of us experience when we begin to ski. David had only to concentrate upon the *postures* that I described. Because skiing is an intellectual sport, because turns work when physical forces are in optimum relationship for controlled changes of direction, and because David listened *precisely* to my advice for effecting those forces, he learned to ski with wide track parallel turns in *one week*! David was blind, but his kind of blindness was easier to conquer than the common blindness of *fear* that many skiers bring to ski class. That kind of darkness is the most formidable deterrent to your progress. Have faith in your instructor. If he is qualified, you need only to *listen* to his commands. He will be quick enough to spot your miscalculations and shout a correction that will prevent a fall, if you will just . . . *listen*.

2. **The Ski**. Before you take off, you should be aware of a few physical principles that will affect your movement down the slope. First, *study the shape of your ski*. Its bottom is flat. If that flatness is allowed to rest completely on the snow, gravity will pull the ski downhill, no matter which way the ski is pointed (Fig. 3-9). The tip, or forebody of the ski is curved upward. This is to prevent the ski from nose-diving into pot holes or bumps (called moguls) as it slides downhill. The curve of the tip is called tip-splay. Skis designed for short radius turns frequently are splayed upward more abruptly than skis designed for longer turns. The forebody of the ski is wider than the waist or center portion of the ski. The width of the tail or rear part of the ski is also wider than the waist, though not quite as wide as the tip. This hourglass configuration forms an arc when the skier's weight presses his skis into a *reverse camber* in a turn and allows the skier to *carve* his turns in the snow rather than skid them (Fig. 3-10). He twists his skis onto their inside *edges*. The edges are steel runners that are embedded into either side of the ski's bottom; they are meant to be kept *sharp* for maximum control. Some skis have one-piece edges, while others are "cracked" at intervals to facilitate the flexible matching of the base of the ski to the changing undulation of the terrain. One-piece edges give a greater *spring* to the ski if a skier bounces on them like on a diving board. Helping that bounce is a bow in the bottom of the ski, called a *camber*. Placed bottom to bottom with the tails and forebodies of the skis touching, a space should exist in the center, (Fig. 3-11), that's the camber. The groove running down the center of the ski bottom helps the ski to track in a straight line; this is especially important when landing from a jump off a bump or cornice. Many *ballet* skiers fill this groove with wax to facilitate 360 degree turns and other trick maneuvers.

3. **Turning With Parallel Skis**. This used to be an *advanced*

maneuver, but if the skis you are wearing are short and your legs are strong, you can point them downhill and *steer* the skis by "axial motion," twisting the feet around the axes of the lower legs early in your learning experience. Your feet and skis are twisted into the desired direction while the skis are *flat* to the snow surface. It will help to *crouch* with your feet separated the first time you try this, in order to lower your center of gravity and provide a broader base of support. If you maintain that "flat ski" attitude after the turn, gravity will continue to pull the skis downhill sideways. That's called a *skidded* turn with a *sideslip* (Fig. 3-12). To prevent such lateral slippage, you are encouraged to tilt your skis onto their uphill edges after a turn when you go across the hill. Tilted onto their uphill edges, your skis will resist the gravitational pull sideways and slide toward the cross-hill direction in which they are pointed. This is called *traversing the fall line*. (The fall line is the line that a ball would take were it allowed to roll downhill.)

For optimum control, your skis should only be *flat* to the snow surface when they are pointed directly downhill or when a deliberate sideslip is desired. Tilting the skis onto their uphill edges is called *edging*. An advanced skier, travelling at higher speeds anticipates his next traverse direction by edging while he is in *the fall line* or even before he has reached that downhill direction. He *carves* his turns on his edges. (Fig. 3-13) The simplest manner of tilting your skis onto their uphill edges is by rolling your knees uphill (Fig. 3-14). The stiff sides of your ski boots will control the tilt of your skis as you roll your knees. If you were to travel across the hill (traversing), with your knees directly over your skis, your ski bottoms would be more flush with the snow surface and a skid to the downhill side would follow. Rolling your knees *downhill* could be disastrous at slow speeds, as this will cause you to fall on the downhill side of your skis! Uphill edging while traversing can be amplified if your hips are also swung uphill, together with your knees. This position is especially advisable for women whose pelvic structure slants their femur bone inward at a greater angle (Fig. 3-15). Such an anatomical variation causes many women, and some men, to ski "knock-kneed." With the uphill knee riding directly over the uphill ski it cannot be edged properly. A swing of the hip to the uphill side of the skis will edge both skis properly when traversing. (Fig. 3-16) To balance this uphill movement of the lower body, your upper body should tilt *downhill*, at least until your shoulders are parallel with the slant of the slope (Fig. 3-17). On a gently graded beginner slope, that tilt will therefore not be very extreme (Fig. 3-18). An important principle for optimum balance when skiing is to *keep your upper body 90 degrees to the slant of the snow beneath your feet at all times*, whether traveling across the hill or straight downhill (Fig. 3-19). An exception to this rule applies to the downhill racer who sometimes assumes a low crouched posture with his torso tipped forward (the *egg position*), designed for maximum acceleration. It is curious that many beginners will crouch and sit back when they are afraid or want to slow down. (Fig. 3-20) This is precisely what a downhill racer does when he he wants to go *faster*! (Fig. 3-20A) With no friction under your ski tips, you will take off like a bullet!

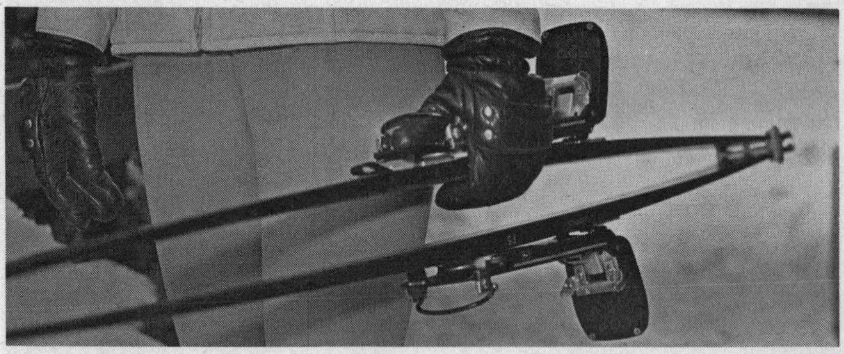

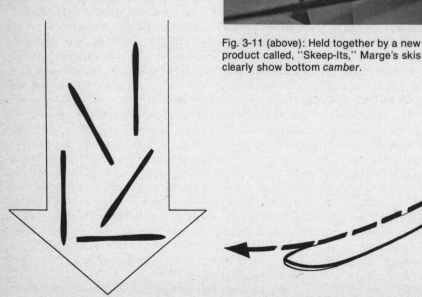

Fig. 3-9 (below): No matter which way your skis are pointed, if their bottoms are *flat to the snow surface,* they will slide straight downhill. That is what is known as *the fall line.*

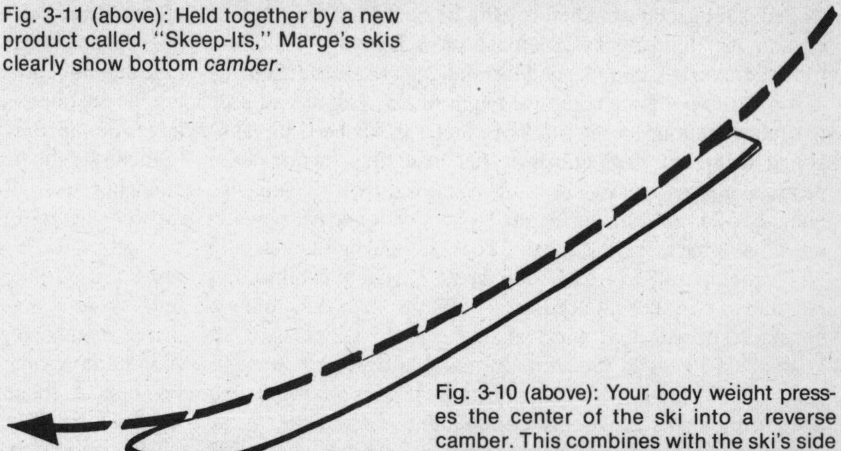

Fig. 3-11 (above): Held together by a new product called, "Skeep-Its," Marge's skis clearly show bottom *camber.*

Fig. 3-10 (above): Your body weight presses the center of the ski into a reverse camber. This combines with the ski's side camber and flex pattern to carve the arc of your turn, if you have twisted the ski onto its inside edge.

Fig. 3-12 (above): A skidded turn on the flat bottoms of your skis may easily be effected by axial motion of the feet, coupled with a down motion for weight release. Don't try it on a steep slope, though!

Fig. 3-13 (right): Carving a turn at high speed after a thrilling run down the Stauffenberg run at Taos Ski Valley, my skis ride on their inside edges. I'm in a traversing posture before my new traverse direction has even been reached.

Fig. 3-14 (below): Tilt of the knees uphill will be followed by a tilt of the skis onto their uphill edges. This will keep your skis tracking in a traverse direction. Note my hip position.

Fig. 3-15: Ginny is typical of many women and some men whose anatomical hip structure causes them to ski *knock-kneed*. Look what happens to her uphill ski!

Fig. 3-16: By reaching uphill and forward with her uphill hip, toward the twigs I've set on the ground, Ginny corrects her problem. Now look again at her skis!

Fig. 3-17: Marge finishes a high speed turn and traverses toward the camera in excellent form. Note how her upper body is 90 degrees to the slant of the slope. See how her hip compensates for her *knocked knees* in order to tilt her skis onto their uphill edges.

Fig. 3-18: My 5-year-old daughter, Cami, traversing in good form. On a more gentle slope such as this, body angulation need not be extreme. Her hip still swings into the hill, and her shoulders are still *parallel to the slant of the slope*. Notice the space under her downhill edges.

Fig. 3-19 (left): Two pros whooping it up on Mt. Norquay's North American run. Note how the torso of each skier remains in a constant 90 degree relationship with the slope.

Fig. 3-20 (above): Sit back and your skis will take off like a bullet! It's your pole baskets that belong behind your heels, not your *derriere*.

Fig. 3-20A (below): Jo-Jay Jalbert, stunting for Robert Redford in the Paramount film *Downhill Racer,* was travelling at about 60mph when the camera froze his accelerating position. Note the air under his ski tips.

Fig. 3-19A (above): Simon Hoyle photo of two skiers on Jerry's Run at Sunshine Village is another good example of the quiet upper body maintaining a 90 degree relationship with the angle of the slope, as the lower body swings like a pendulum and provides the motor force for the turning of the skis.

DR-26-27-107

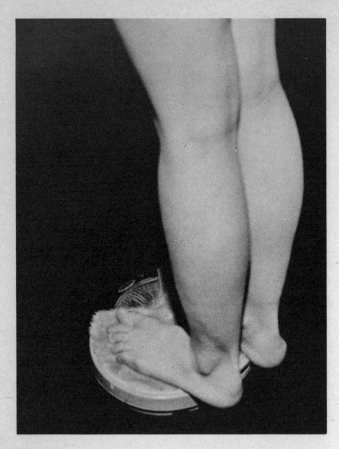

I have mentioned that short skis can be pivoted beneath the feet by axial motion if your legs are strong enough, and that you can help this dynamic movement by lowering your center of gravity—the closer your belt buckle gets to your skis, the easier it will be to twist them (as long as your knees are leading your boots!). Remember that if you ever ski out of control!

4. **Unweighting**. Long skis are difficult to turn by axial motion unless they are unweighted briefly during the initiation of the twist. This *unweighting* can be effected by a sudden *sink down* or an equally sudden spring upwards. Both methods of unweighting can be demonstrated on a bathroom scale (Figs. 3-21 & 3-21A). Most skiers have no trouble understanding how they can minimize their weight on their skis by jumping *up*, but few believe that a similar weight release will take place with a sudden drop *down*. Your scale will prove this. Long skis may also be spun like a propeller when the skier is directly over the peak of a mogul (a bump of snow) with no friction beneath his tips or tails (Fig. 3-22). During the fifties and sixties, it was the practice of advanced skiers to turn on long skis by pivoting on the forebody of their skis while the tails were lifted or unweighted (by a movement of the skier's body *upward* and *forward*). If the forebody of each ski was rolled onto its inside edge it would spoon out the turn as its greater width cut into the snow (Fig. 3-23). The resulting *short swing* was and still is an effective manner of descending steep terrain on long skis. Modern skiers, on contemporary stiff-tailed skis, can unweight and pivot on the *tails* of their skis, but their thighs must be strong enough to pull their weight forward again once their skis are pointed downhill.

Fig. 3-21 (above): This skier weighed in at a hair over 100.
Fig. 3-21A (below): A quick drop DOWN moved the scale needle to 60, proving the most efficient manner of unweighting your skis.

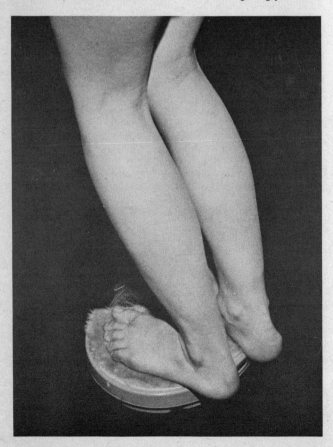

C. EXERCISES ON SKIS

Following is a logical progression of exercises for those who would teach themselves with a pure parallel GLM technique.

1. *Gliding On The Flat*. Your *center of gravity* is just behind your belt buckle. When you stand in your skis on flat terrain with your feet about a hip width apart and all your joints slightly flexed, you will feel stable. Walking on skis differs from walking in shoes in the respect that you will advance most comfortably by *sliding* or gliding each ski forward rather than picking up your ski and "stepping." *Drive* each gliding step with your knee by literally trying to kneel on your ski tip. Right now, get used to leading the toe of your boot with your knee. Never allow the knees to trail behind the toes of your boots if you want to control your skis! Use your poles for balance, holding them as shown (Figs. 3-24, 3-24A), and swing your arms as you would when walking normally, i.e. your left arm swings forward as your right foot moves forward, and vice versa. Study the sequence in Fig. 3-25.

2. *Flat Terrain Step-Around*. With your poles planted on either side of your body and your skis placed together, begin to step around by moving your right ski tip 6 inches away from your left. Then, bring the left tip alongside the right, resuming a parallel relationship. Continue to step completely around. Your ski tails should be the center of your turning circle. Next, try a similar exercise, using your ski *tips* as the center of your turning circle. Replant your poles with each step and weight them forcibly. (Fig. 3-26)

3. *Sidestepping In The Traverse Posture*. The most impor-

Fig. 3-23 (above): I used to advise my students to think about skiing on *the sides of their ski tips*. It is still good advice if you use a longer ski.

Fig. 3-22 (above left): Skis may easily be spun like a propeller if you shorten their *running surface,* as when you stand on the peak of a mogul.

Fig. 3-24: First, put your glove *through* the pole strap.
Fig. 3-24A: Then, grasp the strap and the pole handle.

Fig. 3-25 (below): Glide forward on the flat surface by pushing your knee forward. Don't try to *lift* your ski. Slide it, like Larry, Teri and Steve.

Fig. 3-26 (above): Try turning in place with your ski *tips* as the center of your circle. Keep your steps small.

Fig. 3-27 (above): When your knees are directly over your skis, your skis will be *flat to the snow surface.* They will slide downhill, pulled by the force of gravity.

Fig. 3-28 (below): Tilt your skis onto their uphill edges by rolling your knees uphill. Friction beneath your uphill edges will prevent the skis from sliding downhill.

Fig. 3-29 (above): Lift your poles as you take a step uphill, planting your ski on its uphill edge.

Fig. 3-30 (right): Plant your poles for support each time you transfer weight to your uphill ski and bring the lower ski up to meet it. Note the tilt of the shoulders; they're the same slant as the slope.

Fig. 3-31 (below): The convex part of my lower boot fits into the concave portion of my upper boot. For boots with straighter sidewalls, think about the same relationship in bare feet.

Fig. 3-32: My uphill ski has slid downhill toward my lower ski because my uphill knee is directly over the ski. This is called a sideslip (of the uphill ski).

Fig. 3-33: Starting position for your first *sideslip*. Note that my knees and hips are swung to the uphill side of the skis to keep them on their uphill edges and prevent a slide downhill.

tant position to be learned by the average recreational skier is the *traversing* posture, the stance used for crossing the slope, perpendicular to the *fall line*. The time to learn it is now, as it happens to be the very same position used for optimum balance when you climb the slope in what is called a *sidestep*.

Find a small incline that slopes upward gradually. Obviously, if you tried to climb this hill with your skis pointed straight toward it, your skis would slide backwards. Flat to the snow surface, your skis would be pulled downhill by gravity and the absence of friction between their slick bottom surface and the wet icy snow. It is advisable to climb sideways, but even in that stance, gravity will pull your skis downhill *if they are flat to the surface of the snow* (Fig. 3-27). Tilting the skis onto their uphill edges, you can provide a substantial resistance against that gravitational pull. (Fig. 3-28) Climb uphill sideways taking each step on the uphill edge of your ski. If the snow is fresh, your tracks will look like steps in the snow (Fig. 3-29). The slope I am climbing in these photos would be too steep for the average beginner, but I wanted to emphasize the parallel relationship between the shoulders and the hill. And, I just had to give you a peek at Colorado's Maroon Bell peaks from the top of Aspen Highlands. What a spot!

The simplest manner of twisting your skis onto their uphill edges is by trying to kneel on the uphill side of your skis. Any movement of the knees uphill will be followed by a tilt of the skis onto their uphill edges. Swing your hip uphill also. This is called *edging* via *transverse leverage*. Study Fig. 3-30 for the proper form when climbing or descending in a sidestep. Each time I bring my skis together (between each step), I resume a correct traversing posture with the exception of my poles which are dug in for support. Notice that my hips and knees swing *uphill* while my shoulders are maintained at the same angle as the slope on which I climb. This

is called body *angulation*. What you may not be able to detect is that my uphill ski leads my downhill ski by several inches; in fact, *everything* on my uphill side is leading—my uphill ski, uphill boot, uphill knee, uphill hip and shoulder are all leading slightly. This is an anticipatory posture that will aid your "parallel" turns later on. *Now* is the time to learn it! Each time the skis are brought together, the convex curve of the downhill boot is tucked tightly into the concave curve of the uphill boot (Fig. 3-31). The few inches lead that my uphill boot takes ahead of my downhill boot is the same lead taken by my uphill ski, knee, hip and shoulder. Finally, observe how I plant both poles with each step, for maximum support and balance. Climb up the slope several steps and then walk down, maintaining the same posture and stepping each time on your uphill edges. Perfect your sidestep-traversing posture before you even take your first run, and I guarantee you will be skiing with parallel skis in one week! But . . . be patient!

4. *Sideslip For Edge Control.* You probably noticed while stepping *down* the hill that your uphill ski occasionally skidded a bit as you stepped it next to your downhill ski. (Fig. 3-32) This will happen if the uphill ski is momentarily flat to the snow surface, which occurs when you release the hold that it has on the snow by relaxing its tilt onto its uphill edge. That kind of downhill skid is called a *sideslip*. It can also be done on both skis, simultaneously. Practicing the parallel ski sideslip early in your learning process will develop the basic skill of *edge control*, most essential to skiing proficiency.

Try this sideslip exercise, *now*, before you even take your first run downhill.

a. Stand in a sidestep-traverse posture a few yards up a graded slope (climb up with the sidestep). Your torso should be perpendicular to the slope, while your hip and knees are over the uphill side of your skis (angulation).

Fig. 3-34: A gentle roll of your knees until they are over your skis will initiate your parallel ski sideslip. Note that my hip is still uphill. Allow your skis to slip downhill to your lower planted pole.

Fig. 3-35: STOP your sideslip by snapping your knees sharply uphill. This will tilt your skis onto their uphill edges. Snow will pile beneath your skis and build a wall against the gravitational pull.

b. Plant your poles an arm's distance away on both sides of your body. Be sure to dig in the uphill edges of both skis to prevent a premature slide (Fig. 3-33). Face your lower pole. You are going to sideslip toward it.

c. *Gently* release your edges by rolling your knees directly over your skis. Keep your hips on the uphill side of your skis during this whole maneuver; torso perpendicular to the hill. When your skis are almost flat to the surface of the snow, gravity will pull them downhill and you will skid to your planted lower pole (Fig. 3-34). When you have slid to that lower pole, drive your knees uphill again to bite the snow with the uphill edges of your skis. This action will stop the skid, as the snow bunches up beneath your skis. (Fig. 3-35) You have just performed your first successful *sideslip* and the *hockey stop*. Try it several times, replanting your poles each time, until you reach the flat snow area. Then, turn around in place, sidestep up the slope facing the opposite way, and practice a series of sideslips again, with your skis facing that new direction. *Practice this exercise repeatedly*, until you feel that you can actually control your sideslip with just your knees and edges. Then, try it without planting your poles (Fig. 3-36). Learn to sideslip and stop in both directions before you take your first run downhill. This unorthodox procedure of teaching the sideslip before a straight downhill run is where my approach to ski instruction differs with most other systems. You will soon learn why.

Try to keep your body weight directly over the center of your skis during the sideslip, but keep your hips on the uphill side of your skis and your shoulders parallel to the slope. Once you feel control over this basic skill, climb higher and see if you can sideslip for progressively longer distances. Always stop your slide by driving your knees into the hill sharply, tilting your skis onto their uphill edges. As I mentioned, this will pile up the snow beneath your skis and brake your slide. Be sure to balance yourself by keeping your shoulders slanted to the same degree as the slope throughout this exercise—you will hear me say that a lot, as I believe strongly in the educational value of repetition.

5. *Discover The Effect Of Longitudinal Leverage*. I should remind you, at this stage, that your skis should still be facing *across* the slope. You are not quite ready for your first run with your skis pointed straight downhill. So far, your sliding movements have been down the hill *sideways* via release of your skis' edges.

Because the ball of each foot (just behind the toes) is directly over the center of the running surface on both skis, a movement of your center of gravity forward or aft will be followed by greater body weight pressure on the front or rear of your skis. This is called *longitudinal leverage*, and your ability to control it is another basic skill required of the proficient skier. (Think of your "center of gravity" as a point just behind your belt buckle.)

When you were practicing your sideslip, if your body weight was not concentrated over the center of your skis, you probably experienced a moment of imbalance. If your body weight was *forward*, the tips of your skis skidded downhill faster than your tails; if your longitudinal leverage was aft, the tails of your skis led your sideslip. Both movements will be utilized later in advanced skiing maneuvers. This time, let's be deliberate in our use of the leverage principle:

a. Climb several yards up the slope again with a hard edges sidestep. Assume a good sidestep-traverse posture (angulate), tilting your knees and hip uphill and your shoulder line parallel with the slant of the slope.

b. Release your edge hold on the snow by rolling your knees over your skis and flattening their bottoms to the snow surface. Be sure to not roll those knees too far, or you will catch a downhill edge! Your hips should remain on the uphill side of your skis, at this stage.

Fig. 3-36: Sideslipping is a safe and respectable way for a novice to come down a slope that he has ventured on with poor judgement, like this steep pitch at Taos Ski Valley. Notice how my torso is 90 degrees away from the slant of the slope in this hockey stop.

Fig. 3-37 (above): Begin a sideslip by rolling your knees over your skis. Then, move your hips forward and downhill also. Extra body weight on the front of your skis will assist the gravitational pull. Your ski tips will slip downhill faster than your tails. This *forward sideslip* is the key to your first parallel turn.

Fig. 3-38 (below): The optimum posture for traversing, or crossing the hill, with your skis together. Everything that is on your uphill side should be leading. The hip is swung uphill and the shoulders are parallel to the slant of the slope.

c. As your skis begin to slip sideways down the slope, tilt your center of gravity forward by moving your hips over your boots (maintaining good knee bend, of course). Your extra weighted ski *tips* will automatically slide downhill faster than your ski tails. This is called a *forward sideslip* via hip projection (Fig. 3-37).

d. Still maintaining good knee bend but on the flat surface of your skis to continue your sideslip, tilt your center of gravity backward to weight your ski *tails*. The backward leverage pressure will drive your ski tails downhill faster than your tips. It is called a *backward sideslip*. Your hips are your most powerful motor force. Learn how to use them to your advantage.

e. Alternate forward, backward and straight sideslips until you feel control over the leverage of your skis in the sideslip maneuver. Try it from both traverse directions. Then, you will be ready to ski straight ahead.

6. *Traversing.* Your first forward movement on skis should be *across* the hill, not straight down. (Be patient!) Pick a *concave* slope so that your first traverse will end in an automatic stop. Let's review the optimum posture:

a. If you are in good shape and have good balance, by all means try to traverse with your boots together—the convex portion of your lower boot tucked into the concave part of your upper boot as when you sidestepped.

b. Bent knees and your hip should be swung uphill to tilt both skis onto their uphill edges.

c. No part of your body should trail behind your heels.

d. Shoulders should slant at the same angle as the slope.

e. Everything uphill should lead slightly—the uphill ski, boot, knee, hip and uphill shoulder are all slightly ahead (Fig. 3-38).

f. If your balance is poor or your physical condition is less than adequate, try traversing with your skis apart. Pro-

Fig. 3-39 (left): Steve shows the *wide track* approach. Angulation is less imperative because of broader base of support. Current American Teaching Method used by the Professional Ski Instructors of America favors this approach. I don't.
Fig. 3-40 (below): Marge in trouble. What would *you* advise her as an instructor.

moters of the wide-track approach do not advocate a close boot relationship for the beginner, as they feel that a wide stance is more stable. With a wide stance, the need to angle the shoulders parallel to the hill can be minimized, as body weight is maintained more equally on both skis (Fig. 3-39) and your center of gravity will be above a broader base.

g. Once in a good holding traverse posture, push off with your poles, pointing your skis just slightly downhill to get some momentum. At all costs, maintain a good traverse posture and glide on the uphill edges of both skis, but keep your knees flexible enough to absorb terrain undulation.

h. Problems you may encounter while traversing:

(1). If you are falling on the uphill side of your skis when traversing with your skis close together, you forgot to slant your shoulders the same angle as the hill.

(2). A fall on the downhill side of your skis is caused by catching your downhill edges when your skis are held *too flat* to the snow surface. Traverse on your uphill edges.

(3). If your ski tips separate, your body weight is too far back. Don't *sit!*

(4). If your ski tails separate, you are probably bending forward too much from the waist and one or both skis are too flat to the snow surface. (Fig. 3-40) Minimize your forward waist bend. Rather, traverse with a sidebend, until your shoulders match the angle of the slope.

(5). If your ski tails are skidding downhill, you are sitting too far back. *Always lead your boots with your knees!*

(6). Should your ski tips cross, you probably forgot to lead your traverse with your uphill ski, boot, knee, hip and shoulder. Rather than in a purely parallel position, your skis should glide in a *parallelogram* position. When I teach kids, I tell them to point their belly-button downhill. Try it. It will keep your uphill hip forward. If your downhill hip is back, it will keep your downhill ski back. A ski tip cross almost always will follow an advance of the downhill ski when a beginner is traversing.

(7). If you ski too fast and crash into the woods, you forgot to pick a *concave* slope to slow down your traverse, or you began with your ski tips pointed too far downhill. Try a less steep traverse.

7. *Traverse, Forward Sideslip And Stop!* Once you have perfected your traverse in both directions, link up a traverse with a forward sideslip:

a. Traverse a *convex* slope on your uphill edges. Maintain good body angulation.

b. At the crest of the convex slope, release your edges by rolling your knees over your skis. As your boots pass the peak of the bump, *project* your hips and torso down the fall line. Because of your forward momentum and longitudinal leverage, a forward sideslip should follow. Stop your forward sideslip by sharply driving your knees forward and into the hill. This will tilt your weighted ski shovels onto their uphill edges abruptly. Your unweighted ski tails will skid downhill, and a platform of snow will pile up beneath your tilted skis, eventually causing enough resistance to stop your slide. Some call this form of stopping a "hockey-stop" (Figs. 3-41A, B, C & D).

c. Try this maneuver in *both* directions.

8. *The Fan.* Once you have perfected your traverse, forward sideslip and stop exercise, try it from a steeper traverse; then steeper; then still steeper. Finally, try it from almost straight downhill (Fig. 3-42). This progressively steeper traverse forward sideslip and stop is called *The Fan* exercise. Try it in both directions. You are closer than ever to parallel skiing.

9. **The Downhill Running Posture.** It may seem strange to some readers (my P.S.I.A. colleagues notwithstanding) that I have not spoken of the downhill running position until this time. My reasoning is that a beginner should know how to *finish* his first run before he is taught how to begin it. Too many new skiers push off from the top of the slope with no conception of how to turn or stop. They comprise the greatest number of casualties on the daily accident report; they are frequently unschooled "turkeys" who give a bad name to our sport; but, sometimes, they are just unfortunate learners who have been taught inefficiently. If you have

Fig. 3-41A (below): Begin this exercise with a well edged traverse. Reach for the "X" that I've marked with your knees and your uphill hip.

Fig. 3-41B (right): Start a sideslip while you're traversing by rolling your knees over your skis. Change it to a *forward sideslip* by projecting your hips toward the direction of intended travel.

Fig. 3-41C (left): Stop the downhill slippage by resuming a good traversing posture and driving your knees toward the "X" that I have marked. Your ski tips will then carve a small turn into the hill.

Fig. 3-41D (below): Sharply angulate by driving your knees and hip uphill while you drop your downhill shoulder. The pile-up of snow beneath your skis should result in a complete stop. Some skiers like to punctuate their *hockey* stops with a hard plant of their downhill pole!

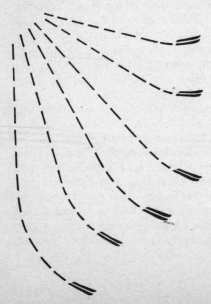

Fig. 3-42 (left): A traverse, forward sideslip and hockey stop usually results in a *turn onto the hill* with parallel skis. Start with a shallow traverse, almost 90 degrees to the fall line. Gradually increase the steepness of your traverse until you are *straight in the fall line*. This exercise is called *the Fan*.

perfected your traverse form when climbing in a sidestep or when skiing *across* the hill, and if you have had a reasonable amount of success with your sideslip and "hockey-stop," you are ready to take your first run straight down the fall line:

a. Assume the proper stance on flat ground first, to study its form.

b. The position of the skis is *parallel* to each other. If your balance is good, lock one boot inside the other, as described in your traversing posture instruction. If not, a separation of 4 to 6 inches between your skis may feel more comfortable. Allow the leading boot to be the one on the inside of your anticipated turn—i.e. skiing straight down the fall line, the right boot leads by a few inches before a right turn, the left boot leads before a left turn.

Most ski schools advocate the wide-track fall line stance for beginners, presupposing that your balance is not too keen and that you will feel more control with a broader base under your center of gravity. This is certainly true in some cases: some people can't even *walk* in a straight line *off* skis; others walk with their toes pointed outward like Charlie Chaplin's memorable silent movie character; still others carry so much fat in their middle and bottom regions that it is virtually impossible for them to *stand* with their feet together, let alone move that way on skis! For those individuals, and for anyone who is inexperienced at other forms of kinesthetic activity, I, too, recommend a wide-track stance.

On the other hand, if you have ever ridden a bicycle, enjoyed running on the beach, ridden a horse, skated, studied ballet, slalomed on a water ski, or even have learned

Fig. 3-43: Marge in a good posture for skiing straight downhill. Be sure to keep your hands *forward* and your knees in front of your boots.

how to walk steadily in a straight line, there is no reason why your first run cannot be in the classic form of a ski instructor—with the convex part of one boot tucked into the concave portion of the other. Lead with your right boot if you plan to turn to the right and with your left boot if you plan to finish your run with a left turn.

c. All body joints should be loosely flexed. If you have purchased a good boot, your knees are already locked into a position that is over the front of your toes, by the forward flexing of your ankles. If you are using Uncle Louie's hand-me-down rocker-soled boots, issued when he skied with the 10th Mountain Division, they are of no help at all, and you will have to *press your knees* forward until they hide your boots.

Drop your seat *slightly* until it is in a line above your heels, (but not behind your heels), and tip your torso forward until it is at the same slant as your lower legs. (Fig. 3-43)

Your arms should be bent slightly at the elbows, while your hands are forward and wider apart than your shoulders. Pretend that you are serving a tray of food to your downhill audience.

Your head should be flexed back to enable you to look several yards ahead. It is not good practice to look down at your skis.

d. While your pole *handles* are kept forward by your extended arms and hands, your pole *baskets* (the pointed end) should trail behind your body, about a foot above the snow.

e. If your skis are shoulder height or longer, your body weight should be concentrated at a point forward of your boots, where it will be if you ski on the balls of your feet (just behind your toes). Pretend that you have tacks under your heels. Don't step on them! If your skis are below shoulder high, and they should be if you are just beginning, distribute your body weight evenly over the entire ski.

f. Assume the correct downhill running posture on flat terrain and rock up and down, flexing your knees several times to accustom yourself to the balance. You might feel the front of your boot pressing into the front of your leg. You should *not* feel the back of your boot pressing into the back of your leg!

g. Next, climb the hill with a good sidestep reminding yourself to angulate, with your knees and hip swung uphill and your shoulders slanted, parallel to the slope, in preparation for your first downhill run.

10. **The Bullfighter Turn.** Once on top of your first practice hill—if you have climbed with a sidestep—you are faced with the problem of turning in place in order to face downhill (the fall line). The method you learned on the flat won't work on a hill, as the moment your skis would face the fall line they would shoot downhill like a rocket! Such a situation calls for the "Bullfighter."

a. Dig your uphill edges deeply into the snow to keep from sideslipping and twist your torso until it faces downhill.

b. Hold your pole handles in the palms of your hands and reach out to plant your ski poles as far away from your body as you can, directly in line with your ski boots but a shoulder width apart—(*Your* shoulders). (Fig. 3-44) Plant your poles and let them support your weight. (Fig. 3-45) There should be a straight line from your pole baskets running through your poles, your forearms and your upper arms to your shoulders. This "locked elbow" position will tax your arm

Fig. 3-44 (above left): Hold the butt of the pole handles in the palm of your hands. You're going to support yourself on them as you turn around.

Fig. 3-45 (above center): Be sure to keep your skis tilted onto their uphill edges as you plant both poles.

Fig. 3-46 (above right): Lock your arms at the elbows and keep them as straight as your poles.

Fig. 3-47 (left): You'll have no trouble stepping around if you keep your steps SMALL.

Fig. 3-48 (right): Marge takes off. She's sitting back a bit, a natural tendency with beginners of skiers who fear fall line. At this stage make a concerted effort to *kneel on your ski tips.* That will keep your body weight forward and your skis in control!

Fig. 3-49: Marge's spring upward and forward lightens her skis' weight burden in preparation for a turn.

muscles less and make use of your arm bones as support (Fig. 3-46).

c. With SMALL steps, step your ski tips around until they both face downhill (the fall line) between your planted poles. (Fig. 3-47)

d. Align your boots, either locked together or in a wide-track stance, so that the right boot is slightly ahead in anticipation of a right turn.

11. **The First Run Downhill.**

a. Flex your ankles until your knees hide your boots and you feel body weight pressure under both feet as you relax your pole support. Ski right through the middle of your initial pole placement and grip the pole handles normally as you continue to slide. Assume the correct downhill running posture that you practiced on the flat. (Fig. 3-48).

b. Fix your eyes upon the spot where you wish to turn and let your skis slide. Rock up and down gently, flexing your knees. Be sure to keep them in line with the toes of your boots. Enjoy the flight. You are in control if your posture is correct

c. Rise up to an almost erect posture, hips forward, knees still leading the boots, body line 90 degrees to the slope when you are ready to turn. (Fig 3-49) Then sink (Fig. 3-50) down sharply, making an effort to *kneel* to the right of your ski

Fig. 3-50: A drive of her knees toward the spot I've marked with an "X" tilts Marge's skis onto their inside edges. Her ski tips spoon out a neat right turn, assisted by the side camber on her skis.

Fig. 3-51: The snow will fly!

Fig. 3-52 (above): Turn completed, Marge assumes traversing posture for a new direction, with her shoulders the same slant as the slope, hip and knees pressed forward and uphill. No part of her body is behind her heels.

Fig. 3-53 (below): Marge in a left traverse. Note the similarity between this excellent traversing posture and the body position used for climbing with a sidestep.

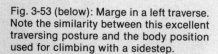

Fig. 3-54: Centrifugal force pulls outside your turn. You must lean away from it or you'll fall to the outside of your turn.

Centripetal force pulls inside the turn. With *angulation* your torso leans away from it and effects an optimum balance for skiers who ski with their skis *together*.

The *wide track* turn will allow you to fight centripetal force by weighting the ski that is *inside* the turn, as we see Marge doing here, with your outside ski functioning as an outrigger for balance. This is called *inclination*.

tips. If you edge sharply enough, the snow will fly! (Fig. 3-51) Twist your boots and knees to the right as you lead your turn with your inside hip and assume a right traverse position to cross the slope. You should have had enough practice traversing to assume this posture automatically. (Fig. 3-52) Its angulated form is designed to combat the power of centrifugal and centripetal forces which seek to destroy your turn.

Remember:

(1). Your torso remains perpendicular to the slope from start to finish. Shoulders should slant parallel to the hill when you traverse.

(2). Knees and hip are swung to the uphill side of your skis in order to edge them while traversing. The shape of the ski will then carve the finish of your turn for you.

(3). Body weight pressure remains on the forward part of longer skis, with the shovels of your skis spooning out the turn. Shorter skis may be equally weighted from tip to tail to prevent a spin-out.

(4). Everything uphill leads when traversing—the uphill ski, boot, knee, hip and shoulder. All are slightly ahead. The precise amount of lead is determined by your boots, as the lower boot locks its convex curve into the concave curve of the upper. (Fig. 3-53) If you are performing this exercise with a wide stance, lead your traverse the same way, but with your skis apart and with less angulation. (Fig. 3-54) Angulation is also less imperative in deep powder snow.

To stop sharply, drive your knees farther forward and uphill as you increase your body angulation, and you will stop with the aforementioned "hockey-stop" by abrupt *edging*, as your unweighted tails skid a few inches downhill.

Try several straight runs and turns to a stop, turning each time in a different direction. Just remember to lead with your right boot and your right hip for a right turn, and your left boot and left hip for a left turn. Body angulation while traversing is crucial if you are turning with your feet together. With a wide-track stance, it is less important, as the body weight is then distributed more evenly over *both* skis, and the broader base of support will even allow some body *inclination* during the turn.

12. **The First Fall And Resurrection.** Everybody falls. If you can accept that, you will have less hangups about falling and place less importance upon how others will react to your errors. The truth is that other skiers will be more compassionate than ridiculing, since they have all been in the same embarrassing position more than once. Falls are less traumatic today than they were 15 or 20 years ago. High modern boots with stiff shanks (if they fit properly) make an ankle injury almost impossible today, and release bindings (properly adjusted and compatible with a skier's boots) are working better than ever to separate the skis from the skier in a potentially damaging fall. Add to this the technological advances of the ski industry and the methodological improvements of the ski schools, and you will understand why accidents have decreased on a per skier comparison since the primitive years of two decades ago.

Nevertheless, you *will* fall. Sometimes, a spill is caused by *collision*—an uncontrolled skier who has never taken a lesson and does not know how to stop or turn crashes into you. Occasionally, a sudden change in terrain condition (ice, chunky snow, a pothole or sitzmark) will cause you to relax your mental concentration upon your form. Any deviation from the form prescribed by your instructor can cause a moment of imbalance and a fall. A *sudden distraction*, like a field mouse dashing across the slope, another falling skier, or a skin tight pair of stretch pants can also bust up your concentration and cause a spill.

I should mention that, during the entire week that the blind boy, David, was under my tutelage, he did not fall a single time! He proved to me that *posture* is the essence of control. David was devoid of the distractions of sight. His posture was perfect. The positions that your instructor prescribes will prevent a fall, but the performance of those movements requires *total* concentration and rejection of any stimulus of distraction. That kind of concentration is available to all but achieved by few. Again, it's a question of *purpose*. If you want something bad enough, you set your sights on it and approach it aggressively in the straightest line possible—like the racer. Distractions are obstacles in your course. David really *wanted* to ski. I provided the prescription. He followed my directions precisely and succeeded. It might have been quite a different story if he was *not* handicapped and more susceptible to harmful distractions.

The worst distraction that an instructor must deal with is *mental preoccupation*. It causes a great percentage of falls. An instructor can spot a potential collision and shout a warning to his student; he can see terrain changes and steer his class away from them; he can stall his instruction for a moment and join the rest of the class in ogling that neat pair of stretch pants that skis by. What he has difficulty discerning is mental preoccupation, a primary deterrent to a skier's learning process: Mary is so frightened to death of moving down that 10-foot slope that she's about to wet her britches; Sam is so overwhelmed by the pretty girls all around that his head is about to unscrew, while his heart rate has jumped to 150; Alice doesn't give a rap about the posture her instructor is demonstrating as she has plans for his evening; George is only in class because his wife insisted. His mind in on the Rose Bowl game, and he'd rather be in his overstuffed chair in front of the TV with a good cigar. These students will retain little of what their instructor describes as optimum balance positions. They will fall.

Fortunately, the good Lord gave us a fine cushion to absorb the shock of inadvertent falls. The problem is that many of us don't use it. Our first movement, when a fall is imminent, is to reach out and block the impact with our hands. This can result in a fractured ulna, a dislocated thumb, a crushed bursa, or, at least, a sprained wrist. *Use that cushion.* It's located in the seat of your pants. That round thing that's got cleavage. If a fall is inevitable, stick out your seat and cushion the impact. At the same time, try to get your boots together but thrust your skis *away* from your body (Fig. 3-55). If you are on a steep slope and you begin to slide head first down the fall line, do everything you can to spin around and get your skis *below* your body and pointed across the slope. The edges of your skis are your best brake to stop that kind of a slide. Beginners need not worry, as the slope on which you practice should not be very steep. All skiers should stay away from steep terrain when wearing slick shiny clothing. That material is faster than your skis, and a fall on the steep could be disastrous! I lost a student who wore an outfit like that for a class on Stein's

Fig. 3-55: Marge takes a bummer. She'll be all right, though. She's using her cushion!

Fig. 3-56: Bring skis up close to your center of gravity, and be sure that your skis are pointed *across* slope.

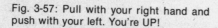

Fig. 3-57: Pull with your right hand and push with your left. You're UP!

Run, at Sugarbush Valley. She made one turn, miscalculated, fell, slid and didn't stop until she'd bounced from mogul to mogul, all the way to the bottom!

Forward falls are dangerous. Avoid them. If you feel one coming on, swing your seat to the uphill side of the slope and *sit!*

Now, you have done it. You have fallen for the first time, and the other seven people in your class are impatiently waiting for you to get up. At least, that's the way it will seem to you. You will feel like the dunce, and your adrenalin will boil! In the face of that embarrassment, most men will rise up by brute force. But, some men, and most women, are not brutes. They have to use their intelligence. They must reason that it is foolish to try to rise when their skis are pointed downhill, as gravity will then simply make them slide farther. Whichever way you may have fallen, your first rising effort should be to swing your skis until they rest *across* the fall line, in a traverse direction. Some fallen positions require the skier to roll over on his back in order to swing his skis across the hill. The wise skier then *uses* gravity and the dependable assistance of leverage in the following manner:

a. Bring your boots and skis up close to your seat.

b. Dig in the uphill edges of your skis. Deeply.

c. Take your hands out of your pole straps and hold your poles together.

d. Dig in your pole tips all the way to their baskets, close to your uphill hip. Hold your poles just above the baskets (the rings) with your uphill hand—firmly. (Fig. 3-56)

e. Place your downhill hand high up on the poles on top of the handles, if you can reach that far.

f. Pull with that downhill hand, push with your uphill hand, and let gravity do the rest as you stand. (Fig. 3-57)

There are other methods, but this is by far the most successful. Unless you fall on flat ground. If you spill on the flat and you are not muscular enough to pull yourself up (as gravity will offer you no assistance), either release the binding from one of your skis and step up, or swallow your pride, blink your eyelashes and ask for some assistance. Most skiers will be happy to help you. Now, let's get back to skiing.

13. **Graduating The Length Of Your Ski.** After a day or two of practicing the exercises I have just mentioned, trade in those rented arm-pit-high skis for a pair that are shoulder-high and practice each of the 12 exercises you have just learned for a least an entire day. I know you are anxious to link your turns, but the longer you wait, and the more you practice the exercises for development of the basic skills that I have outlined—edging, sideslipping, leverage, traversing, straight running and the "hockey-stop"—the easier it will be for you to link several turns together.

On the shorter ski, you probably felt more in balance with your center of gravity directly over the middle of your skis. With a longer ski, you should move that center of gravity to a point forward of your boots. This is easy if you tip your torso slightly forward until it is at the same angle as your lower legs *and* ride on the balls of your feet, just behind your toes, feeling little contact under your heels. In either case, your knees should hide your boots, so press them forward (if the shape of your boot doesn't place them there for you) and *keep* them there! (Fig. 3-58)

14. **An Easier Way Up.** It is a bonus for learning how to turn and stop. Up until now I have had you climb the bottom of the slope with the sidestep. You probably looked with envy at the hundreds of skiers who have been riding the chairlift next to us and wondered why I have put you through this torture. Two reasons. The first is that I want to condition your reflexes to automatically assume a good angulated posture when your skis face across the hill. If you have climbed repeatedly in that traverse posture (on your uphill edges, with your knees and hip swung uphill and your shoulders slanted parallel to the angle of the slope) between each of your practice runs to a sideslip and "hockey-stop," the chances are good that you will automatically fall into that position every time your skis point across the fall line. Secondly, most chairlifts require the skier to stand and ski down a gentle slope while his chair continues to move. A lift operator is usually stationed at the point of disembarkation to pull back the chair while you stand and push off. What would you expect to do at the end of that run if you could not turn? Probably what 80 percent of uninformed beginners do at the end of their first chairlift ride: stand, slide, crash and burn! Now, you can ride the lift with less apprehension, confident that you are at least capable of skiing down that narrow run when you leave your chair and making one turn or a stop. Find yourself a fox and do it! (Fig. 3-59)

15. **First Parallel Run From The Top.** You have ridden the chairlift for the first time, slid down the exit ramp and successfully turned. A short walk or sidestep has brought you to the top of the novice slope. Over a thousand feet of downhill skiing awaits you. You look down. It scares the hell out of you. You can push off forgetting all I have taught you and pray that you don't embrace a tree or another skier. You could take off your skis, ride the lift down and give up this insane sport forever. Or, you can remind yourself that it was not too long ago when another beginner stood in your same spot, thinking carefully about what his instructor had to say, pushed off and got to the bottom without falling. And . . . he was blind. . .

Let's review a few basic principles:

a. A ski will slide downhill (the fall line) if its bottom is flat against the surface of the snow, no matter *which* way the ski is pointed. Skis should be totally flat to the snow surface ONLY when skiing straight down the fall line or when deliberately sideslipping.

b. A ski that is flat to the surface of the snow can be easily turned by axial motion (like a propeller) by steering it with the feet and legs, IF THE KNEES ARE DIRECTLY ABOVE THE FRONT OF THE BOOTS! Skiing straight down the fall line, try to hide your boots with your knees.

c. Axial motion of longer skis is facilitated by an unweighting effort. This can be a sudden *down* movement flexing all body joints, a spring of the body *upward*, or a shortening of the skis' running surface, as when the skier stands on the apex of a mogul or when he pivots on his ski tips or ski tails.

d. Your skis will track *across* the hill if they are tilted onto their uphill edges, as a platform of snow will form beneath them and provide resistance to the pull of gravity downhill.

e. Edging (tilting the skis onto their uphill edges) is best accomplished by pressing your knees forward and to the

Fig. 3-58: Larry turns his short boards very well with his body weight pretty well centered. Longer skis, like mine, need more weight pressure on the forebody, achieved by tipping the torso forward slightly and skiing on the balls of the feet, just behind the toes.

Fig. 3-59: Teri and Steve going up the easy way at Aspen Highlands.

uphill side of your skis; it may be amplified by swinging your hip uphill also, but keep your balance by dropping your downhill shoulder toward your downhill heel, until your shoulders slant parallel to the angle of the slope (body angulation).

f. Parallel skiing is safer skiing although the boots do not necessarily have to be locked together. If your balance is good, your form will be more graceful in a locked boot relationship; if this is your choice, lock the convex portion of the inside of your downhill boot into the concave curve above the arch of your uphill boot. The uphill ski should always lead the downhill ski by a few inches while traversing, as should the uphill knee, hip and shoulder.

g. It is possible to ski downhill sideways by simply releasing the hold of the uphill edges when the skis are in a

53

traverse attitude. This is called a sideslip. It is accomplished by rolling the knees over the skis to flatten their relationship to the snow. *Some* bite of the uphill edges should be maintained even when sideslipping, to prevent a catch of the downhill edges and moment of imbalance.

h. A sideslip may be terminated by a sudden tilt of the skis onto their uphill edges. Snow will then pile up under the skis and provide a formidable resistance to the pull of gravity downhill. This is frequently called a "hockey-stop." The sudden tilt of the skis is accomplished by a sharp drive of the knees uphill, coupled with body angulation to maintain equilibrium.

i. Longitudinal leverage toward the shovels of the skis will change a sideslip into a *forward* sideslip, with the shovels sliding downhill faster than the tails. Longitudinal leverage behind the heels will cause the ski tails to slide downhill faster than the shovels into a *backward* sideslip. Body weight should be centralized when sideslipping directly down the fall line, not forward nor aft.

Concentrate upon those nine principles as David did and forget about the visual stimuli of fear that confront you. If your form is accurate, you WILL succeed, as he succeeded. Your first run should be no more than a series of short downhill slides, turns to traverses and hockey-stops. Don't try to link together right and left turns. Not yet. You will be ready for that next lesson after you have completed a perfect run, practicing only the straight downhill position, the sideslip, the traverse and the hockey-stop, in *both* directions.

16. Linking Parallel Turns.

a. The Forward Sideslip. Find a steep slope and practice your sideslip. If your body weight is centralized while sideslipping you will skid *straight* down the fall line although your skis are pointed across it. You learned that a short while ago. Move your center of gravity forward and that straight sideslip will turn into a *forward* sideslip (your ski tips will skid downhill faster than your tails). This is the link between your parallel turns! Perform a series of linked straight and forward sideslips. Be sure to lead your sideslip posture with everything that is uphill—the uphill ski, boot, knee, hip and shoulder should all lead by a few inches, just as before.

b. The Change of Lead. From a holding traverse close to the fall line (Fig. 3-60), move your knees and hips over your skis and forward into a forward sideslip and *switch your leading ski, boot, knee, hip and shoulder* (Fig. 3-61). That subtle exchange, performed when the skis are flat to the snow surface and pointed close to the fall line, will facilitate the axial motion that is necessary to cross the fall line. Axial motion should begin with a downward drive of the knees into the new traverse direction. (Fig.3-62) Pressure applied to the tips or shovels of your skis, once they are tilted onto their uphill edges, will continue the arc of your turn. Once you reach the traverse line that you want, move that pressure back and ride the entire ski. Your angulated posture will automatically place more body weight on your downhill ski. Check your traverse form. Are your skis on their new uphill edges? Are your knees and hip swung uphill? Do your shoulders parallel the angle of the slope? Are the uphill ski, boot, knee, hip and shoulder all a few inches ahead? Practice the forward sideslip and change of lead in both directions. Now you can link your long parallel turns.

Fig. 3-60: Begin a steep traverse, just barely off the fall line. Note my body dynamics.

Fig. 3-61: Start a forward sideslip into the fall line by moving your hips and knees directly over your skis and *forward*. Now, change your leading ski, knee, hip and shoulder. Note the neutral position of my shoulders when I am skiing straight down the fall line.

Fig. 3-62: My knees and left hip tilt *inside* the turn away from centrifugal force. My right shoulder drops to fight the pull of centripetal force. My skis carve, and I am in perfect balance.

Fig. 3-63: Pole plant near the ski tip, when traversing at an extreme angle to fall line, must be followed by a vigorous effort to swing tails into the fall line.

Fig. 3-64: Planting the pole *in the fall line* will effect a faster turn with less effort, especially if the pole plant is followed by an anticipatory movement of the torso *downhill*.

17. **Pole Action And Anticipation.** Up until now you have read no mention of the poles other than my suggestion to keep their baskets trailing behind with their handles forward. The poles are relatively superfluous in the early stages of your learning process. Some GLM schools even take them away from beginners. I don't, because my beginners are encouraged to sidestep up the hill a lot, and pole support makes climbing easier. Poles also come in handy for rising from a fall. Now, we will see how they can help you turn.

Most parallel skiers prepare for a turn by planting their downhill pole in the snow. Many of them don't know the best spot to plant it. If the pole is planted close to the tip of the downhill ski when traversing, a strong effort must follow to swing the ski tails into the fall line (Fig. 3-63), as the pivot must take place under the shovels of the skis. This kind of vigorous turn was popular in the fifties.

The French, spearheaded by champions like Killy, Russel and Augert, taught us that a parallel turn could be made faster and with less effort if the downhill pole is planted *always in the fall line*. Thus, in a traverse that is 90 degrees to the fall line, the downhill pole is planted to the side, (Fig. 3-64), directly below the skier's body, allowing him to pivot his skis like a propeller under his boots, or if acceleration is his intent, on his ski *tails!* (Fig. 3-65)

In either case, the purpose of the pole plant is to trigger the deflection and the *projection* of the torso upward and forward *toward the fall line*. This dynamic thrust is called *anticipation*. The movement of the upper body downhill is soon followed by an uncoiling of the lower body and thus the skis. This is an automatic physical assist to the axial motion

Fig. 3-65: A pole plant in fall line allows me to *anticipate* my turn by moving my torso toward it. When the upper half of my body is blocked and can't twist any farther, the lower half will follow its lead. I can than pivot under my boots or on my ski tails! *Note change of my leading ski.*

Fig. 3-66: Preparatory phase. Torso faces intended direction of travel as pole is planted in fall line. A knee push uphill should create a "pre-turn" into the hill.

Fig. 3-67: Turn initiation takes place when torso twist is blocked and lower body uncoils to recover neutral position. Body projects 90 degrees to the slope angle, leading ski is exchanged and knees will now drive forward to place body weight on the forebody of the skis.

Fig. 3-68: Turn execution is continued by twisting knees, feet and skis via axial motion, as my hip swings into the hill and my outside shoulder drops to match the angle of the slope.

Fig. 3-69: Turn completion is simply a resumption of the new traverse position. Note how my knees and hip swing to my right, causing my skis to roll onto their inside edges.

of the skier as he pivots his feet into the new direction. It is the primary reason why I believe that even the beginner should ski across the fall line in a parallelogram, i.e. with his uphill ski, knee, hip and shoulder all leading his traverse.

Here we go:

a. Traverse in good form on a wide gentle slope.

b. Without changing your posture, advance your downhill pole basket (the ring), and freeze it, 6 inches above the snow.

c. Plant the downhill pole in the fall line with a sharp drive of your knees uphill. Such a movement will create a "pre-turn," as your shovels turn uphill and your unweighted ski tails push downhill. This will check your speed, as in a hockey-stop, giving you a platform of snow beneath your skis from which you can spring up and into the fall line. (Fig. 3-66)

d. Spring up and move your hips *forward*, projecting your upper body and both hands downhill as you flatten your skis; this should trigger a momentary forward sideslip (Fig. 3-67), as your legs uncoil to catch up with your torso. Immediately *change your leads*, pivot your feet, and sink down driving your knees forward and into the new traverse direction. (Fig. 3-68) Check your traverse form again. Is everything uphill ahead? Are you gliding on your uphill edges? How is your body angulation? (Fig. 3-69) Try a similar turn in the other direction.

e. Practice this turn from different angles of traverse, always planting the pole that is INSIDE THE TURN downhill, then springing like a cat into the fall line as you flatten your skis and change your leads. Deflection or rebound from a platform of snow created by a "check" along with the pole plant can be explosive if the skier severely angulates and applies strong lateral downhill pressure on his skis at the moment of the pole plant. Snow will fly and the resultant uncoiling of the lower body as the torso moves downhill is frequently accompanied by a lifting of the ski tails. The pivot in this classical type of parallel turn is under the tips. The final movement of every turn should be a drive of the knees and uphill hip forward toward the new traverse as the body angulates. As you improve, the change of edges and leads will be so rapid, it will appear that your skis are never flat to the snow surface. This is the classical manner of turning with "parallel" skis.

18. **The Easiest Parallel Turn Of All.** The last exercise is the traditional method of turning with your skis together, bouncing off a platform of snow that develops under your skis after an abrupt pre-turn uphill coupled with a pole plant. Every platform is a check of your speed, as in a "hockey-stop," which among its practical benefits provides a psychological security for the timid skier who does not feel comfortable skiing at high velocities. There is another type of skier, though, and another type of parallel turn. For the racer, the speed freak, for you who are lured by the thrill of speed, there is the easiest parallel turn of all. It employs *inclination* as opposed to *angulation* but may also be combined for a very graceful, totally secure high speed turn.

a. Start in a traverse in good form, knees and hips swung uphill, shoulders parallel to the slope, body weight mostly on the lower ski if the snow is hard packed or shallow, or on both skis if the snow is powder or deep and heavy, (Fig. 3-70) then, begin a forward sideslip. (Fig. 3-70A)

Fig. 3-70 (above): From a good holding traverse, on your uphill edges. . .

Fig. 3-70A (below): . . . move your hips and knees forward and over your skis to initiate a forward sideslip. Your skis should flatten to the snow surface, and your ski tips should drift toward the fall line.

Fig. 3-71: When your ski tips have drifted 45 degrees away from your initial traverse, *incline* your body *downhill and forward*, planting your pole at about two o'clock to your direction of travel. Be sure to stay forward by standing on the balls of your feet.

b. Rise up to an almost erect posture, tilting your *entire body* about 1 o'clock to your direction of travel as you plant your pole at 2 o'clock. This upward and downhill movement will trigger a flattening of your skis to the angle of the hill and the forward leverage of your body weight will continue to push your tips downhill faster than your tails in an accelerated forward sideslip. (Fig. 3-71)

c. Assist the inception of your turn with axial motion of your skis as you change your leading ski. This should head you straight down the fall line with your body 90 degrees to the angle of the slope. (Fig. 3-72)

d. Continue turning your skis by applying pressure to their shovels with a kneeling motion, forward and in the direction of the turn's completion. This should roll the forebody of your skis onto their inside edges and spoon out the completion of your turn.

e. Now you have a choice. Follow with a traverse and good *angulation,* or tilt right into another *inclinated* parallel turn. (Fig. 3-73) The choice depends upon the direction of travel you desire next. With no setting of the edges or platform position, this type of turn is designed for high velocity, minimum physical effort and maximum courage. It functions beautifully on a Giant Slalom course and on a western type slope where you have plenty of room and not too many obstacles in your path.

19. Moguls (Those Bloody Bumps) And Avalement. Ask the majority of new skiers what is their greatest fear. Half will say steep slopes while the other half will answer "MOGULS" as they hunch their shoulders and quiver their lower lips with apprehension. Moguls are menacing to most novices who have finally become comfortable performing their early training exercises on relatively flat beginner terrain. Some are shocked to hear that ski areas actually design their slopes to deliberately include bumps for the pleasure of advanced skiers. It is true. The better you get, the more you will seek "bump runs" for the variety of challenge that they provide.

A deep groan was heard through the entire Mad River Valley of Vermont last week when a new type of "Snow-Cat" called a Kassbohrer Pisten Bully crept down one of the steeper bump trails at Sugarbush Valley called The Mall, crushing all the moguls in its wake. For years, that trail was an arena for the best of skiing's gladiators, who could be seen in competition with each other every weekend for top gun status. It was well known that no one but the very best could negotiate that entire narrow trail of sheer-faced moguls, which divided the men from the boys, without making at least one miscalculation. A friend of mind suffered a compound fracture from a slam into one of the towers on the Mall. He died two days later. The Mall was Sugarbush's answer to Al's Run at Taos, although not as long. What makes it as interesting is that the Valley House chairlift passes directly above its entire length, and skiers have a front row seat to some of the finest skiing in the entire Northeast! The Pisten Bully turned the Mall into a ballroom carpet last week. Its weekend athletes were replaced by stem turners almost as soon as the machine chewed up its first run. Turkeys were strewn all over the trail. Sad. If this continues, Sugarbush mogul busters will have to move next door to Glen Ellen's "Scotch Mist," a very similar trail, or be content with hidden challenges like Stowe's "Goat," an hour northeast, which have no critical audiences overhead. This is one bump lover who sincerely hopes that they keep the Piston Bully off "Stein's Run." If they don't, more Sugarbush Valley skiers will follow its former Norwegian ski school director to the Rocky Mountains where the needs of athletes are as respected as the comforts and limitations of lesser skiers, who should ski on trails designed for their particular level of ineptitude. I hope they never get a Bully on "The Rumble!"

Moguls are not fallen skiers who have been snowed upon. Not usually. Curiously, it is the less proficient skier that usually is the creator of a mogul. His hesitations, doubts and fears are generated to his skis which then cut up new snow into a maze of small valleys and humps. The valleys are his erratic tracks where he has scraped off the surface snow

Fig. 3-72 (left): When your skis point straight down the fall line, *drive your knees forward* as if you were trying to kneel on your ski tips. When you can't get your knees any farther forward, push them toward the inside of the turn and tilt your ski tips onto their new uphill edges. The shovels of your skis should spoon out the right turn's completion as you ride on your inside edges.

Fig. 3-73 (right): Finish your turn by resuming your traverse posture, or incline into a left turn as I'm about to do here. The arrow points to the direction of my next inclination—forward and downhill.

This inclinated turn is designed for high speed; at a slow speed, this inclination in the downhill direction can catch your lower edges and cause a serious fall.

clear down to the icy base. The humps, bumps, or *moguls* are built up piles of that scraped off surface snow which grow taller and taller as more less proficient skiers follow the same cautious line. Adding insult to injury, the short ski aficionados have destroyed the pleasurable large round bumps that made runs down trails like the Mall so rhythmic and graceful a decade ago. Characterizing most eastern bump trails today are short choppy bumps with little space in between, sharp rises and icy faces where the short-ski skiers have checked, pivoted and skidded, scraping all the snow off the downhill side. Accepting the adage, "If you can't lick 'em, join 'em," most veteran skiers have traded in their long boards for a shorter pair of sticks. While we miss the long rhythmic turns over the bumps of the fifties, we welcome the challenge of the new terrain, which demands quicker foot work and a sound knowledge of the modern mogul mashing technique known as *avalement*.

It is a French word that we are told means "to swallow." The reference is to the "swallowing" of the bump as the skier retracts his knees and feet to pivot on the crest of the mogul. The movement requires strong *anticipation* or drive of the upper body downhill after the customary pole plant in the fall line, as the initiation of the turn finds the skier with his hips in a seated position and his ski tips in the air pointed in the traverse direction. With the upper body facing downhill, it is twisted to a maximum variance with the hips and legs. The pole provides stability and deflection as the lower body then uncoils like a twisted rubber band, spinning the skis toward the fall line, assisted by axial motion of the skier's lower legs. Projection of the upper body 90 degrees to the angle of the slope, as the legs are extended into the valley on the other side of the mogul, gets the ski tips back in contact with the snow, and a quick roll onto his uphill edges keeps the skier angulated and in total control, as his legs are extended in the valley beyond the mogul.

Study avalement from a traverse in slow motion:

a. Approach the mogul from an angle 45 degrees to the general fall line of the trail in a good traverse position, with the basket of your downhill pole swung forward for planting. (Fig. 3-74)

b. Roll your knees in a plumb line with your boot toes, as you shoot your boots forward and retract your knees to swallow the bump. (Fig. 3-75) This will lessen the weight pressing down on your ski tips and permit them to climb the bump with no shock upon contact. (Fig. 3-76)

c. When your boots reach the top of the mogul, twist your skis downhill and onto their inside edges, EXCHANGING YOUR LEADING BOOT, as you tilt your torso downhill and plant your downhill pole. (Fig. 3-77) Your turn will be carved on the inside edges of your ski *tails*.

The bite of your inside edges should not be affected by a lateral thrust, but rather by a FORWARD THRUST. Some skiers call this movement *jetting*, as the skis will accelerate. It is possible to shoot the boots and skis so far forward (flat or on their downhill edges) that only the ski tails will be in contact with the snow for that precarious moment when you must twist your knees and feet toward the fall line. This is called a "wheelie." (Fig. 3-78)

What saves you from a fall immediately after that seemingly unbalanced position is the same procedure for completing an avalement turn:

Fig. 3-74: Preparation for avalement is your basic traverse position with pole basket advanced, ready for planting. Note how my shoulder slant matches the tilt of the slope.

Fig. 3-75: The moment of avalement is when I "swallow" the bump by retracting my knees and jetting my boots forward. Note how my torso begins to move downhill, but maintains a 90 degree relationship to the slope.

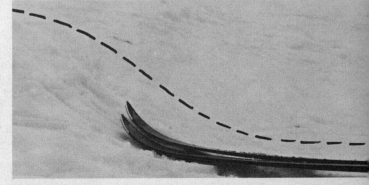

Fig. 3-76: Weight release off ski tips will allow them to climb and snake *over* the mogul instead of tearing *through* it.

Fig. 3-77: An important part of the anticipatory movement is the change of the leading ski before the skis have been turned into the fall line.

Fig. 3-78 (above): It's a "wheelie" and it's a neat turn, but you need powerful thighs and tough knee ligaments to finish it! I've changed my leading ski and am about to roll my knees inside the turn.

Fig. 3-79 (right): Avalement completion. Body moves upward and forward to press ski tips back into contact with the snow. Once they point downhill, I resume my traversing posture, extending my legs in the valley below the mogul. *Note how my shoulders resume parallel relationship with the slope. This keeps the torso in a constant 90 degree angle to the hill.*

1. Your pole plant on the downhill side of the bump which gives some support.

2. Your upper body projection downhill (anticipation) *90 degrees to the slant of the slope.*

3. The extension of your legs into the valley beyond the bump as you angulate into your new traverse direction. *The torso remains perpandicular to the slope.* Observe the completion in triple exposure. (Fig. 3-79)

The final part of your avalement turn over a bump is just as important as its inception. It is a resumption of that very same posture you learned in your early lessons—the angulated traverse position. Remember, though, that mogul may have a steep downhill face. If your turn has taken you perpendicular to the fall line, drop your downhill shoulder until the angle of your shoulders *matches* the slant of that face! This action will balance the angulation of your knees and hip *uphill* and prevent you from falling on the uphill side of your skis, seduced by centripetal force.

Be sure to keep your hands always forward and your torso facing downhill when skiing a *narrow* moguled trail. This will help your anticipatory projection. Since your movement down a narrow trail will allow no traverse, you can forget about dropping your downhill shoulder. With your torso facing the fall line, you will have no downhill shoulder. I tell my students: The torso is quiet and perpendicular to the slope, whether you are skiing straight downhill or across the hill. *If you have a downhill shoulder, drop it.* Toward your heel. Advance your pole basket with just a flick of your wrist and don't hang on to your planted pole too long, or it will throw off your timing.

The very same principles may be applied when skiing over smaller bumps although the retraction of the knees and feet is naturally minimized. The idea is to keep your head at about the same level above the snow through the entire course. (Figs. 3-80A, B, C & D) Do remember to retract your knees and *jet* your boots forward when you climb the bump. Do tilt your upper body downhill immediately after that jet

Fig. 3-80A (left): Marge spots a small rise with a steep drop beyond its ridge. Avalement may also be used in a situation like this.

Fig. 3-80C (above): There's a slight flaw here, but I'm going to print it anyway, because the rest of her form is neat. Can you spot it? She forgot to advance her inside ski. With the outside ski leading, a tip cross is imminent. Fortunately, Marge was quick to correct, as you can see in the next photo.

Fig. 3-80B (above): She pulls up her knees and shoots her boots forward, planting her pole in the fall line. With little of her skis on the snow, her pivot will now be easy.

and drive your knees forward into the new traverse direction, as you advance your outside pole basket in preparation for the next bump.

20. **Wedeln.** It is an Austrian colloquialism for "tail wagging" which hasn't been too popular since the freestyle movement came on the ski scene, but wedeln is a classic form that will always be part of the proficient skier's repertoire. Explained simply, it is a linked series of short parallel turns straight down the fall line with no traverse. Edging takes place but only briefly at the termination of each axial motion of the parallel skis. The upper body is kept QUIET. All body joints are flexed as in the downhill running posture described in Exercise 9, but the bend at the waist is less appreciable. The hands are kept forward, spaced a bit wider than the shoulders, and one pole basket is always forward, poised for planting, while the other trails behind. The tails of the skis follow the advance of the pole basket as they are thrust downhill by axial motion when the skier twists his knees and feet away from the fall line. The pole is planted in the fall line as the knees drive to the uphill side of the skis. This triggers a spring upward and forward as the other pole basket is advanced and an axial motion in the opposite direction takes place. Here is wedeln, step by step:

a. Begin a run straight down a *gentle* slope. Assume a slightly taller than usual downhill running posture. Keep both hands forward, pole baskets behind. (Fig 3-81A)

b. Advance your right pole basket with a flick of your

Fig. 3-80D: A dynamite finish! Look at those inside edges bite!

Fig. 3-81A: Upright for a classic Wedeln.

Fig. 3-81B: Imagine your ski tails connected to your pole basket. As you advance the basket, bring the ski tails along with it, gently brushing the snow.

Fig. 3-81C: Remember to plant the pole by bending your knees forward and away from it.

wrist, and sink down slightly to unweight your skis, twisting your knees to your left and thrusting your ski tails downhill simultaneously, with your skis relatively flat to the snow surface, as when performing a forward sideslip. Keep your torso motionless. (Fig. 3-81B)

c. Freeze the right forward pole 6 inches above the snow. Then, plant it with a drive of your knees forward and to your left. *Plant the pole by bending your knees.* Don't plant it with an arm movement! (Fig. 3-81C)

d. As soon as the right pole touches the snow, spring up and forward to your original tall downhill running position, simultaneously advancing your left pole basket as you twist your skis back into the fall line. (Fig. 3-81D) Change your leading ski and swing the right pole basket back as you advance the left one. Only one pole basket should be forward at all times in wedeln. The poles flick like a pendulum with just wrist movement. Keep your hands forward.

e. Continue to twist your skis with your knees and feet as you sink down and ready the left pole for planting. (Fig. 3-81E) As before, plant it with a drive of your knees forward and, this time, to your right. (Fig. 3-81F) Notice the change of leading ski!

f. Continue the movements rhythmically, with no traverse interruption, straight down the fall line. Keep your upper body quiet and do all the turning with your knees and feet on relatively flat skis. The only edging that should take place is a brief setting when the pole is planted. Remember to spring upward and forward after each pole plant, simultaneously advancing the opposite pole basket. (Figs. 3-81G, 3-81H)

21. **Short Swing.** Still the safest, most controlled method of

descending a steep packed slope, (Fig 3-82) is the *short swing,* another classic maneuver that will outlive all the worm turns and shoulder rolls of modern free-stylists. Essentially, it involves a pivot under the shovels of the skis and a hard setting of the edges as in the "hockey-stop." (Fig. 3-83A) The ski tails are then lifted (Fig. 3-83B), shortening the running surface of the skis to just the area under the shovels, and the skier pivots on his ski tips pulling his tails back into the fall line. (Fig. 3-83C) The skis regain snow contact when they just cross the fall line and a skid of the tails downhill follows as the skier presses his knees forward and uphill of his planted pole. (Fig. 3-83D) Another hard setting of the edges creates a platform of snow beneath the skis from which it is easy to bounce into the next turn. (Fig. 3-83E) You should feel a tension between your ski tails and your pole basket in the short swing. As the left pole basket is snapped forward by a flick of the wrist, the tails of your skis should come with it, thrust downhill on your left side, etc. (Figs. 3-83F, G & H)

This is the safest and most cautious way to ski super steep terrain, except in deep powder or on icy slopes, as every turn is a sharp check in your speed (almost a *stop*). Practice it on a moderate slope. Then gradually apply the maneuver to steeper and steeper terrain. You will appreciate the control, and, when spring arrives, and the only snow left on the trails is a catwalk 8 feet wide on the sides, *you* will be skiing!

22. **The Windshield Washer.** Do *not* use a short swing as described in deep powder, as your ski tips will dive and you will nose over! When the snow is deep your pivot must be moved back from the shovels to a point under your heels. In such a case, your spring upward from the "check" or

Fig. 3-81D: Every turn is followed by a rise UP and FORWARD to the original neutral position in the fall line.

Fig. 3-81E: The tails follow the advance of the pole basket.

Fig. 3-81F: The pole is planted with a knee bend. Note how quiet Marge's torso is. Motionless.

Fig. 3-81G: The neutral position.

Fig. 3-81H (above): Wedeln is a beautiful way to descend a gradual slope. Remember to keep your torso facing downhill throughout this maneuver.

Fig. 3-82 (right): The short swing came to my aid many times in the Bugaboos, as when I had to chop my way down this steep crevassed slope near one of the spires.

Fig. 3-83A: Each "check" or setting of your edges is like the "hockey stop" you learned as a beginner.

Fig. 3-83B: Bounce off your platform of snow and pivot on your ski tips. Note my change of leading ski and quick advance of the outside pole basket.

Fig. 3-83C: Pole ready, I will plant it with a drive of my knees forward and to my left.

"platform" position should not be forward but should be *straight up*, lifting your entire skis off the sunken base and pivoting them by axial motion (like a propeller) near or above the snow surface with just your knees and feet. The pole action, synchronized with the tails of your skis, remains the same, i.e. as one pole basket is advanced, the tails of the skis are drawn downhill with it. Another difference in this type of short swing, called by some a *"windshield washer turn"* is that the pole is planted to the side rather than close to the downhill ski tip, in an effort to keep the body weight of the ski centralized and *on both feet.* The spring upward is not an elongation of the body as when springing off a diving board. Instead, it is a retraction of the knees and feet. As with most types of skiing exercises, the knees are maintained directly above the front of the boot, although the center of gravity (a point behind your belt buckle) is moved back to centralize your body weight. You should feel like you are jumping your turns with *equal* weight on both skis, as if you were on a pogo stick!

23. **Stem Or Wedge Turns.** A more primitive method of changing direction on skis is by steering with *independent leg action.* This can take various forms, of which the *snowplow, wedge* or a variety of *stem* turns are the most basic. From a holding traverse position (hips and bent knees tilted uphill, shoulders parallel to the slope, no part of the body behind the heels), the skier spreads (stems) the tails of one or both skis. If just the uphill tail is "stemmed," this is called a *stem turn.* At least, it used to be. Every few years, new terms spring up for the same old forms. This year, we are calling the form a *wedge.* This movement points the skier's outside ski toward the fall line. By applying more body weight to the front of that stemmed outside ski and

steering it with his knee, the skier will turn, with the provision that his inside ski remains flat to the snow surface and is unweighted. (Fig. 3-84) Modern schools advise twisting *both* knees into the intended new traverse. This will automatically flatten the inside ski and twist the outside ski onto its inside edge. The American Teaching Method encourages a sequence of foot steering, leg steering and aggressive leg steering in this type of wedge shaped maneuver. The snowplow, wedge or stem position is favored by non-athletic tyros who feel more secure over the broader wedged base. The maneuver is a standard discipline in the manuals of ski schools which teach the American Technique, although, at present, it is referred to as an *early basic christie,* when linked with a sideslip after the turn. It is rejected by schools employing the pure Graduated Length Method technique, a system in which the new skier is encouraged to use short skis and turn *parallel* by axial motion right from the beginning of his learning experience. As the GLM learner progresses, he is encouraged to use a longer pair of skis. The pure Graduated Length Method has had phenomenal success in some areas, but it is not necessarily a faster way. I do believe that this method is safer, though.

At Sugarbush Valley, several years ago, we decided to test the results of both systems. Half the beginning "skiweekers" were taught by GLM, using only *parallel* turns, and half were taken through the traditional ATM sequence of snowplow, stem turn, stem christie and parallel exercises. At the end of the week, there was no significant difference between the skiing ability of those from either group, but several twisted knees and charley horses were reported by those who were taught the awkward wedge or snowplow

Fig. 3-83D: Remember to plant your pole with your knees, not your hand!

Fig. 3-83E: As I bounce, my leading ski changes, and my left pole basket is already on its way forward.

Fig. 3-83F: Still airborne, my ski tails follow the advance of my left pole basket.

Fig. 3-83G: Regain contact with the snow when your skis are at about a 45 degree angle to the fall line of the slope. Have your downhill pole ready for planting!

Fig. 3-83H: By planting your pole with a sharp drive of your knees away from it, you'll get a good bite with your inside edges. *Note how no part of my body is behind my heels!*

posture. That ski week contingent numbered only about 150, hardly a number for conclusive evidence but high enough to cause wonder and radical conjecture.

24. **Special Techniques For Snow Variations.** Included in this segment of Exercises should be a cursory examination of techniques that are applicable to different snow conditions, as these will require constant adjustment of physical attitude:

a. *ICY CONDITIONS.* Beginners should avoid days like these. Might be a good occasion to try yourself out at cross-country or stay in bed with a good book or someone. The *langlaüf* trails are usually cut through beautiful wooded areas that have better snow conditions than the scraped off *piste* under the chairlift. Icy conditions are not for beginners.

No reason for advanced skiers to shy away from these conditions, though. It can almost be enjoyable. There are two ways for a parallel skier to ski icy or boiler plate conditions. I have read in *Ski* Magazine (January 1976, p. 25) that Dixi Nohl, of Mad River Glen Ski Area in Vermont, prefers a flat ski method, riding both skis and powering his turns by forward projection. Forward projection of the body is essential, but it can also be done on one ski, the lower ski, weighted from tip to tail and on its uphill edge, like an ice-skater, with far more control. This movement is called *Schrittbogen* (step-turn) by my Austrian friends. The theory is that all your body weight on one edge will cut a deeper incision into the ice than if your weight is dispersed over both skis. I favor this method. It also demands strong *angulation* (tilt of the lower body uphill and the torso at least 90 degrees to the angle of the slope; while the hips and legs lean away from *centrifugal force* (the force that pulls outside the turn), the torso must balance the skier by dropping downhill, away from *centripetal force* (the force pulling inside the turn). Schrittbogen is an advanced maneuver for parallel skiers—as the downhill pole is planted, lift your downhill ski tail and project your body toward the fall line in

a long arc, turning on the inside edge of your outside ski. The shape of the ski alone will carve your turn. Avoid any *lateral* slippage and make full use of your ski's *side-camber!* Resume your extreme angulation while your skis point down the fall line in anticipation of the new traverse, but keep the tail of your new uphill ski off the ground until you are ready for another turn. (Fig. 3-85) All edging on ice should be via *glissement* or forward projection. Use no side pressure, as you might use when checking or in a "hockey-stop."

b. *POWDER.* It can be up to your boots, knee high, waist high, or, if you are lucky, bottomless. Beginners should shy away from the latter three conditions. Wait until the "cats" pack it down. Here are a few tips for more advanced skiers on how to master the deep.

Boot top-high powder requires no change in your standard form; skiing just becomes more enjoyable. Deeper snow demands alert compensation, however, with disastrous results if you don't adjust. Stiff, long skis will tend to nose dive in the deep stuff, unless you plane them upward by applying more pressure to your heels. You will soon tire, though. It is a lot easier on shorter, more flexible skis, as your body weight will bend your boards into a reverse camber. The slightest roll of your knees in the direction of your intended turn will tilt that arc, and the shape of your skis will finish your turn for you. Skis must be parallel and held tightly together in deep powder, of course. Some powder freaks like to add an up and down motion to this knee action, porpoising their turns by steering with their knees when the skis are floating near the snow surface, but a constant low hip posture, called by some *submarining,* is just as effective, although you need thighs like oak trees! Because the angle of the snow beneath the skis is perpendicular to the skier's body in deep powder, he may bank his turns with *inclination* rather than angulation. It's a floating sensation.

Many skiers think that one must *sit back* in deep powder—don't. Your knees should always be leading your boots in *any* snow condition for optimum steering control. It is true

---

Fig. 3-84: For WEDGE or SNOWPLOW and STEM TURNS, think of your skis as arrows. One is pointed to your right; one is pointed left. The "arrow" that carries most of your body weight will move forward in the direction toward which it points. As with other types of turns, it is the outside ski that should carry more weight; a good reason for *dropping the outside shoulder,* contrary to current ATM and C.S.I.A. methodology. Angulation is so important, I believe that it should be taught in the early stage of your learning process.

Fig. 3-85: Unorthodox as it may sound, the *downhill* ski tail is lifted at the moment of the pole plant. It is kept off the snow until you have crossed the fall line. *Schrittbogen* is an effective method for skiing icy conditions.

that a lower hips position is effective and pressure on the heels as your toes curl upwards will help to plane your ski tips upward, but never allow those knees to trail behind your boot toes, or you will lose control of your ski tips and drown in the white stuff!

Try to ski close to the fall line when the going gets deep. If you should have to traverse, stay over the center of your skis and be sure to weight then *equally*. Equal weight is an absolute prerequisite to controlled skiing in deep powder. Plant your pole in the fall line and tilt your torso toward it as you roll your knees inside the turn. Once you face the fall line, try to stay in it, linking one turn after another. This rhythm can be easily triggered by advancing your outside ski pole basket to lead every turn. (Fig. 3-86) One pole basket should always be visible as the other swings back. Your arms may be more to the side than forward which will keep your weight centralized. A forward arms posture as recommended for packed snow conditions would move your weight forward, causing a nose-dive. Be sure to keep your skis tightly together. Imagine yourself skiing on a single board rather than on two. Try your best to keep your mouth shut. Most of us forget that last piece of advice and scream in orgasmic ecstasy, but an open mouth will soom be choked with powder and it could spoil a neat run.

Finally, ski the deep stuff, but don't *rape* it. If you can't handle it, don't go up there, unless it is with a qualified instructor. The tracks you leave behind will be your personal signature. If that signature is a scrawl you might get tarred and feathered by the powder freaks in your lodge. They are an extraordinary breed and their terrain should be respected.

That's it. Your accelerated course for successful parallel skiing. The time it takes you to perfect each exercise, from gliding on the flat to absorbing the moguls will, of course, vary with each.reader, in accordance with your ability to respond to my directions. One of my students, a professional hockey skater, mastered the whole course in 2 weeks. I learned to ski via the Arlberg system and didn't make my first parallel turn until 3 whole winters had passed!

Of course, there is a great deal more science to the total skiing experience than what I have outlined. Sophisticated extensions of the basics I have provided, like "jetting" or the various racing step-turns, plus aerial and ballet maneuvers would be your graduate education. Take your lessons from a qualified man. Unfortunately, the terms *qualified* and *certified* are not always synonymous. The qualifications of a good ski instructor can be read in the satisfactory progress of his students. Observe your instructor in action before you sign up for a lesson with him. Talk to some of his students, if you can.

If your balance is not too keen or your physical condition is a bit less than adequate, by all means learn via the traditional wedge or snowplow method. Its merits have certainly. been proven. The pure parallel system I have illustrated is a radical departure from that method, but it also has proven itself in the success of my own students. It is worth a try. Any skier who learned to ski following the traditional snowplow, stem, stem christie, parallel christie, and wedeln final forms will tell you that the snowplow position is a very difficult one to lose once you are in the habit of calling upon its security. The truth is that the wedge stance should never be thought of as "a way to ski." Rather, it should be used as a teaching device early in your learning experience (if at all) and discarded as soon as possible. *There is no more dangerous way to ski than with one ski pointed directly across the other*. If you should fall with your skis in that position, your chances of incurring a fracture are far greater than if you should fall with your skis parallel and together. I especially shudder when I see children coming down a steep slope with their knees locked, their derriere back and their skis in the snowplow form. You might think it looks cute, but there is nothing cute about a fracture, and no child would stand a chance if he hit an obstacle at high speed with his skis in that awkward position. Nor would you stand much of a chance in the same predicament. This chapter was for you. Chapter 5 is for the safety of your child.

Fig. 3-86: Quick advance of the outside pole basket is a must in powder. Note how my ski tails follow that advance as I push my knees to my left.

Chapter 4

IN SEARCH OF THE BEST

ONE CURIOUS characteristic of pleasant dreams is that they cannot be precisely repeated. I am certain that you must have had at least one you would like to rerun. Most of us have had more than one, but for many they are forgotten as quickly as they suddenly had appeared. Not so with nightmares. They can be annoyingly recurrent. During my college days I enjoyed some extracurricular acting with a group called Playshop. For 5 years and beyond I had a recurrent nightmare. I would be center stage before an audience of thousands. The leading lady has just cued my line . . . and I am speechless. I have not only forgotten the line; I have forgotten how to speak! And the audience is waiting. That awful nightmare still occurs now and then, but, I have never been able to recall pleasant dreams. Pleasant dreams are curiosities of our subconscious that sometimes function as subliminal satisfaction of unattainable desires. In that sense they are valuable, vicarious experiences, without which some people could not carry on the perfunctory activities of their rather dull lives.

Skiers—real skiers—have little taste for sublimation in any form. They prefer to fabricate the substance of dreams and live them, quite consciously. On or off the slopes. They are performers rather than spectators, and, given the choice, they would rather go to the mountain than have the mountain come to them, via movies, television and other mediums which motivate spectators to dream. A bonus is that we can quite easily recall the pleasant dreams we have lived; all it takes is the desire and the dollars for the unavoidable but, all things considered, moderate cost. Thus it is that Marge and I have returned to our favorite dream called the Bugaboos—the wilderness ski area that is part of the Purcell Mountain Range in British Columbia. Uphill transportation is by Bow helicopter. Here is truly the most challenging and most beautiful downhill ski terrain in the entire world. If you are a fanatic skier, you *must* come here. Beg, borrow or steal the bucks for the cost, but come here. You will never forget the experience,

Guide Pierre gives instructions to the group on how to locate a buried Skadi. Avalanche survival is the first lesson you'll get in the Bugaboos, from teachers who have been there!

Boarding the helicopter in stretch pants and ski boots will be your first athletic accomplishment. Shirley Bridges calmly awaits the vertical lift-off.

cause ten other anxious skiers will be flying with you in the helicopter, and they will expect you to ski down in time for the next flight up. They will also expect your turns to design a neat rhythmical track pattern down the fall line and will be quite annoyed if you rape the mountain leaving sitzmark scars. You will log a minimum of 80,000 but more likely over 100,000 vertical feet of tough downhill skiing in one week. It is possible to log twice that much if you ski with the *first group*. Heli skiers at the Bugaboo Lodge are divided into three or four groups, dependent upon their proficiency. On the first day, you tell them how good you are. On the second day, they tell you how good you *really* are. My advice is to ask for the last group. It is always nicer being promoted than being put back a class on the second day.

My next recommendation is primarily for eastern or midwestern skiers who are used to skiing on hard pack, boiler plate and ice. You probably have chosen a good slalom ski for most of your skiing. That is a wise choice for the kind of recreational skiing you are used to. The advice is—leave them at home. A slalom ski, with its narrow waist and wider shovel, is precisely the kind of instrument that you *don't* want for helicopter skiing in wilderness terrain. Since the shovels of slalom skis are wider, they tend to dig into the deep snow when you change your edges, then they dive for the bottom. You will compensate for this by sitting back, and once you do that your skis will take off like a rocket. A few hours of this awkward compensation might be enough to strain your lateral collateral ligament beside the knee, and that could wreck your entire week. The kind of ski you need for wilderness skiing is soft, wide waisted and waxed! For the deep and steep, if you are new to this experience, I would also advise getting a pair of skis 10cm shorter than what you have been using. At the Bugaboo Lodge they rent such skis for a very nominal cost. These include K2's and one model I have been using this week (after straining that bloody knee ligament on my favorite Head slaloms), the Rossignol Salto. A few other good brands for wilderness skiing are the Lange softstyle, the Head Outback and the Truckers.

and I suspect you will be uneasy until you can afford to return. This invitation is directed toward experienced *skiers*. Please, don't come if you have any doubts about your courage or about your ability to turn a pair of skis continuously for at least 50 turns through deep powder, crud, old wet snow, on avalanche prone slopes, through glades of pines which reach out at you with bare ominous limbs, on slopes that exceed 45 degrees, or between two fresh new steep snow slides which have stopped momentarily to allow your descent and dare you to fall. And don't come if you are shy or apprehensive, be-

Ed Bamiling looks pensive as our Bow helicopter searches for a challenging powder run.

Don't expect to be taught how to ski the wilderness slopes that you will find in the Bugaboos. The guides are accomplished, serious craftsmen who take great pride in their knowledge of wilderness terrain, avalanche avoidance and survival techniques. They have no patience for anyone who expects them to also be ski instructors. They are rugged individualists, each with a distinct personality, ranging from calm and gentle to downright arrogant. Some are especially intolerant of picture takers, so be sure to let your guide know of your intentions before you select your group.

There is in fact not much difference between the skiing style you will use on these precipitous slopes and the style to which you are accustomed at your favorite lift serviced area. The changing of edges is still knees controlled, your bodyweight should still be centered, anticipation or movement of your uphill hand in the direction of your turn still is effective for wide turns. There are, as far as I have been able to determine, only two things which are decidedly different. For skiing deep snow your body weight should be dispersed *evenly* over both skis and your hips should sink a bit lower. If, in deep snow, you were to weight only your outside ski in a turn, as you certainly should on hard-packed terrain, it would sink lower than your inside ski. This would throw you uncontrollably off balance and might result in a tip cross! Keep your weight equal over both skis. Dropping your hips lower will make turning a lot easier as your power will be closer to your skis. Feel the front of your shin pressing against your boot tongue, but curl your toes up to plane your soft ski tips upward. Only when old snow gets heavy should you place more weight on your heels each time you plant your pole. And remember to plant it in the fall line, no matter which traverse line your skis might be taking. Start every new run with both skis pointed downhill. If you have ended a set of turns in a traverse direction, stop, lift your lower ski and dig its tail straight into the hill as you point it downhill so that the front of the ski is in the air; then step your other ski around and dig it into the hill in a similar manner. Drop your tips to the snow and begin turning immediately, driving your ski tips through each turn with a push of your knees. Keep your boots together; *tightly* together for the most controlled and beautiful skiing. Try to pivot close to the snow surface, then drive the tips again with your knees. Lead all your turns with your ski tips and avoid any lateral checking motion. Keep your torso motionless at a 90-degree angle to the slope, and face downhill at all times. For breakable crust, try the old stem christie or even a snowplow turn before traversing and plane your ski tips slightly upward. Go as slowly as you can by completing your turns. For "crud" or old junk snow that has become like solid

The first run will be your most thrilling if you're not used to skiing wilderness. When the chopper takes off, you'll imagine you're on top of the world. The silence among those peaks is awesome.

(Left) Spring snow sticks to ski boot bottoms. The first sound you'll hear interrupting the tranquility is the scraping of boot bottoms against the skis.

(Below) Then, you're off, with miles of untracked snow beckoning. The first powder might be waist deep.

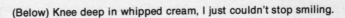

(Left) John McColl Jr. marks the outside of our track pattern with a rhythmic set. He powers his turns with his hip.

(Below) Knee deep in whipped cream, I just couldn't stop smiling.

You'll luck out if you get Tierry for a guide. He likes to take time to admire the scenery while you click off a few photos to renew this precious memory.

snowballs, jump your turns around, but lift the entire ski so as not to allow the tips to dive. Don't fear the deep and steep. You will travel downhill a lot slower in deep snow, and you will feel an exhilaration and freedom you have never imagined.

Take the time to look around when the helicopter drops you on one of the hundreds of peaks that are part of the Bugaboo complex. To hell with impatient guides, you are paying for this experience, and it should be considerably more than a race to the bottom. To the left you might see a towering granite spire spearing through the snow that streaks its base and blends into a virgin, white blanket of 2 square miles, inviting your rhythmic ski tracks. To the right, you see several not so tall jagged peaks completely covered with snow and looking like sharks teeth biting the indigo sky, skirted by a canyon 3 miles deep which has become a bowl of rolling slopes and gulleys that spills white zigzag channels through the dark pine tree line below. Look again. There is an avalanche. Listen to its roar becoming louder as it thunders toward a resting place! Behind you, 50 miles to the north, a billowing cumulus cloud gets dark gray in its belly and bursts, excreting tons of new snow into another valley. At first, it

seems that nothing can be alive here. Then a bold cruising eagle tips its wings and swoops down to see who has dared to invade his primitive territory. Elsewhere, particularly close to the tree line, there are tracks—rabbit, puma, elk and ermine. There *is* life here, and you are about to become part of it. Push off. For the first time in your life, you are *really* skiing. No piste markers. No man-made trails. No noise of lifts or Pisten Bully machines packing the runs. It is just you, the guide, your friends (you will make new ones quickly as there is a close bond formed between those who share dangerous challenges) and this marvelous incredible, high altitude wilderness! There are no superlatives that can accurately describe it. You must experience it.

What kind of people come to the Bugaboos? Here is just a brief report of the variety that we found here this Easter week:

Bill Pitt and his wife Margaret are from Invermere, British Columbia. Bill was the best skier in group three. His wife is quite capable, but a bit apprehensive. Her gentle feminine character will probably never summon the aggressiveness Bill shows when he attacks a new slope. Yet, after skiing, Bill is surprisingly gentle and soft-spoken himself. A forest ranger by profession, he is one of the few men I know who has preserved a good deal of the pioneer spirit in his life-style. The Pitts grow their own vegetables, and they shoot their own meat during the incredibly long and bountiful British Columbia hunting season. He walks to work and back and likes to occasionally run and sprint. The Pitts' favorite recreation is hiking and camping in the same mountains they have chosen to ski. One of the exciting runs we skied together is called Home Run which Marg says is covered with a thick blanket of colorful flowers in the summer. Marg Pitt was hit badly with arthritis about 4 years ago. She still takes "gold shots" or myocrisine every 3 weeks for the condition but feels that physical activity has been the greatest panacea, with skiing heading her list of favorite forms of exercise.

John McColl is 26, bearded and appears a little spaced out when you first meet him. You soon learn that he's high on *life* and living it closer to natural standards of value. John decided to spend a week in the Bugaboos to surprise his father whom he hadn't seen in a while. John, Sr. is a regular visitor at the Bugaboo Lodge who, though over 60, still can tear up a snowfield, leaving a wake of beautiful rhythmic tracks behind. He has logged over a million vertical feet of skiing in this mountain range. He was very entertaining, a bit lecherous toward the ladies and remarkably strong and vigorous. John Sr. even followed the younger men for a skinny dip in the icy creek behind the sauna after skiing on Friday. He runs a foundry in Stony Creek, Ontario. John Jr. spent the last 3 weeks on a camping trip from the state of Washington to British Columbia, through the demanding Cascades with an expedition outfit called Outward Bound, along with nine other trekkers. He has a Bachelor of Arts degree in economics and is an expert in solar energy. John is especially interested in reviving national interest in dirigible transportation for energy conservation. He is an accomplished skier who never once skied ahead of John Sr. and showed a refreshing admiration and affection for his dad.

Tilo Shadrack was born in Berlin. He is mostly self-educated, quite thoroughly, I might add, and owns two hotels, one in Dusseldorf, and one in Arosa, his favorite town, which has about 3,000 inhabitants three seasons out of the year and about 20,000 during the ski season. One can ski to the lifts

Robin Adams and Bill Durlacher take a breather while we lunch over a mile high. Bill came all the way from London for this memorable week!

from Tilo's hotel in Arosa! He has invested his money wisely and now spends most of the year traveling and experiencing new adventures—all funded by rental income! He loves discotheques and the cosmopolitan air of New York City, but would never live there as his taste for the outdoors and clean air is too strong. As a "world resident," Tilo finds Americans quite friendly, more so than Europeans, but if he ever had to "settle down" he would choose Europe, because of the colorful variety of cultures that are in such close proximity. He is a German racing car champion and has driven many Jaguars and Lotus' to victory. He thinks that helicopter skiing in British Columbia is the best in the world!

Mario Pfeifer is a 33-year-old, long-haired Adonis from Weisbaden, Germany who owns a discotheque called "Candy" along with another handsome giant of a youth called Tony. Together they traveled with four other friends whom they have known since they were children thousands of miles in search of wilderness skiing with no restraints. The Germans heard about the Bugaboos in Stern Magazine and are impressed by its vastness. They have skied together frequently in Europe and agree that nothing can match the wild Purcell range of British Columbia. Their trip was arranged by Dr. Pepi Erben, former student world champion racer, who now runs a travel agency called Aero-Ski Reisen in Bad Homberg, Germany, near Frankfort. One of the men in the group, Bernd, is married and has an 8-month-old daughter. These boys were the life of the party at the Bugaboo Lodge Easter week! All very fast skiers, they comprised group two of the heli-skiers, and it was a real pleasure to watch them ski in carefree abandonment, always smiling, friendly toward everyone and a true inspiration to any guest who lacked their

Lunch over, our wingless bird arrives to fly us to another peak. Beside Marge is the young group from Germany. They were very fast skiers.

exuberance. Mario managed to spring off two cornices for a couple of terrific jumps. He skis like a dancer with very loose graceful movements. All the Germans were magnificent physical specimens. To take a sauna with them was like waiting in the wings for a Mr. Universe contest! Tony pushed for a dunk in the crystal clear creek after the sauna and we all complied, with the girls at the Lodge cheering us on. I remarked to my wife how extraordinary it is that people can feel like such good friends after only one week together. It was reminiscent of being in the Army, and I suspect that the closeness comes from sharing such an exciting, challenging and always dangerous adventure together. We all exchanged addresses on the last day and I am certain we will meet again.

Robin Adams, 32, married with two children, is a tall brilliant economic consultant who presently resides in Philadelphia. He came to the Bugaboos with his cousin, Bill Durlacher, from London, also early 30s, good looking Errol Flynn type, who has an infectious laugh. Both boys have heavy British accents, lending another note of color to the quite international atmosphere at the Lodge. Robin was born in Sussex, England. His mother was a proficient skier who was in Olympic training in 1948. She introduced Robin to skiing at the age of 14, and he has done most of his skiing in Switzerland, after his early training at St. Anton. Extensive skiing in Europe and through the eastern and western United States has led Robin to believe that "eastern areas are far more demanding in their physical design, while western areas are more vast and forgiving, European areas are more relaxed and

You'll learn to lash your skis and drag them to the helicopter to avoid contact with its blades.

John McColl Jr. looks apprehensive as his intrepid father reminisces over a million vertical feet which he has skied in the Bugaboos.

You may never ski the same run twice. You will always make a new track. This is the ultimate recreational ski trip — the ultimate high.

Kathy Schindelar, lawyer from Vail, shows Marge and us where the damage is. She skied with an ace bandage, a good deal of pain and a smile from ear to ear.

casual with their 2-hour lunch breaks and sun deck syndrome, and the skiing here in British Columbia is the best in the world, bar none.''

Kathy Schindelar makes her home in Vail, Colorado, where she practices law. Baby faced and ultra feminine, Kathy pulled up to the Canadian Mountain Holidays office early on departure day wearing a plaid skirt, turtleneck and cowboy hat complemented by a dazzling smile which stretched clear across her face. In her mid-30s and certainly attractive, Ms. Schindelar has somehow eluded the marriage scene, probably from dedication to her career, and the resultant independence has permitted her to fulfill her life with many extraordinary adventures. This is not the first time she has tried wilderness skiing, nor will it be her last. A knee injury tried its best to spoil Kathy's week, but she would not submit to the excrutiating pain until it became unbearable. Sitting out a few runs, Kathy savored the incredibly beautiful landscape and drank in the air which could not be as pure anywhere in the world as it is in the Purcell Mountains, far from any form of industrialization. Transplanting herself all the way from cosmopolitan New Jersey to Vail was a courageous move for this young lawyer, and apparently not a lucrative one, according to Kathy. She is contemplating a move to Salt Lake City, where business might be better and good skiing is in the backyard. Of helicopter skiing in the wilderness, Kathy says, ''It is real skiing. Anything else . . . all lift serviced 'skiing' is only a pre-course . . . preparation for the real thing.'' Kathy cuts a neat track, is very bold and positive in her skiing style and showed amazing courage zipping through the forest where the trees were very close.

Because late storms dumped tons of new snow in the entire region over a precarious base that had already begun to loosen from the hot spring sun, avalanche and crevasse dangers persuaded the guides to lead us through more ''tree skiing'' than they normally would at this time of the year. Steep trails like one we enjoyed a few years ago called Anniversary Peak, had threatening cornices which might have given way just at the sound of the helicopter. Only last year, while checking out the terrain for the safety of other skiers two guides were buried in a slide. One managed to radio for help and a fatality was avoided. The guides are well trained for every emergency and the 30-pound pack that is part of their uniform includes vital rescue equipment. No skier is permitted to even ride in the helicopter before passing his Skadi test. The Skadi is a beeper pack that has a transmit and receive switch. While skiing, your pack is switched on to *transmit*. For the test, a transmitting Skadi is buried by the guide, and by switching your Skadi to *receive* and plugging in the ear piece you must find the buried device. You have 7 minutes to find it and dig it out! That is considered a safe period of time for a buried skier to survive, though skiers with strong hearts and healthy cardio-respiratory systems are known to have survived up to 20 minutes under avalanche compressed snow. Needless to say, the test will give you great anxiety, but when your companion skiers are quick to find the Skadi, you will feel a little more secure. Another thing happens. When you all become aware of the vital interdependence that can determine life or death, a unique bond will form between you. What follows is the unique sensation of enjoying a free natural adventure together, or *togetherness in the world of alone*, like marriage should be, I guess. When one skier asked our guide, Pierre, if he ever gets bored giving new heli-skiers the Skadi test, he answered, "No. It might be me who is buried . . ." Pierre was the guide who *was* completely buried for 20 minutes last year and miraculously survived.

Risking the possibility of turning this report into one of biographical sketches, I should like to continue to mention just a few more, as you might then be convinced of the wide variety of skiers who are attracted to heli-skiing, and a reflection of yourself in one of these reports might convince you that the time has come for you to become another courageous customer of Canadian Mountain Holidays' helicopter skiing. It is the criterion of the skiing experience.

Joe Fenkel is a young executive from Philadelphia. We discovered that we had a mutual friend in the enterprising Charlie Brown of the renown Sugarbush Valley. Joe is president of the McClean packaging corporation. His partner thinks Joe is "crazy" to take a week off and ski in British Columbia. Joe thinks the business will survive. His wife

Joe Fenkel's perspiration is a testimonial to the fact that we were working. In one week you can expect to ski over 100,000 vertical feet. If your guide is a pusher, you'll sweat!

encouraged him to make this trip, as she knows how much Joe loves the ski scene. He has schlepped the whole family for weekends in Vermont often enough to appreciate long ski holidays, preferring St. Moritz to other European ski areas for the "total experience" and Sun Valley to other stateside ski areas for the same reason. Of the Bugaboos, Joe just says "un- . . . believable—The best. It beats all," and with that his eyes light up like headlights and his smile stretches from ear to ear. Joe was a big help to me when I hurt my knee on the first run

No photo can describe the magnitude, the sweet silence, the contrast between rugged granite peaks and virgin blankets of snow. This one comes close.

Sometimes it was deep and heavy . . .

Sometimes it was sweet . . .

. . . and sometimes it was mellow.

(Above) Back at the lodge, first stop after a shower and sauna was this table, always amply stocked with fresh oranges. The book is a wine list.

(Left) Marge completes a non-stop plunge down the mountain in good form.

and was visibly upset with my resultant skiing performance. "Hey," he smiled. "Forget it. You don't have to prove anything to anybody. Just look around you. Enjoy it. This is paradise . . . and we're here!" I did look. For as far as I could see, in every direction, there was nothing but deep blue sky and snow. Hundreds of miles of sharp peaks, glaciers and spires. Ahead of our skis, 5,000 vertical feet of unbroken powder, knee deep and light; a world of whipped cream, and a helicopter waiting on the valley floor to take us up to another peak, another boundless blanket of pure white velvet with shadows of powder blue. We both smiled and no words can describe our emotions at that moment.

Bob Seidel is another physically superior business president from King of Prussia, Pennsylvania. His company is Automatic Timing and Controls, an electronics company making industrial controls for machine and process automation. Bob has skied over 43 years, all over the world. He rates the Bugaboos as the most exciting, most challenging skiing experience in the world (where have we heard that before?!). He rates it so highly because of its vast variety of terrain, because it is most physically demanding, because it provides the ideal lift facility. Bob skis only about 30 days out of each winter, but he selects his areas with discretion. His favorite European area is Val d'Isere, with Ernie Blake's Taos, New Mexico ranking number one on his list of great ski areas in the United States. Of mistakes people make in skiing the Bugaboos, Bob notes that over-compensation is number one. "People think you have to sit back in this stuff. Try it, and your skis will run away from you. I stay right over my skis and steer with my knees." Bob is a strong skier who likes to run

and play squash when the snows melt. He has skied just about every well known ski area in the world and agrees that the Bugaboos are "the ultimate skiing experience."

Bugaboos skiers are not all business executives. The preponderance of them and of other professional men and women is due to the steep cost. Who else can afford to drop two grand for a week of wilderness skiing? Some young men and women trade service at the Lodge for their week. The chambermaids are the best women skiers I have ever watched. Ed Bamiling, 30 and sporting a magnificent beard, is a creative master of ceramics who makes his home in Banff. All of his 13 years of skiing has been in the West. He is a guest of one of the girls and has chosen to sleep outdoors on the deck of the service lodge. Ed's a fine skier who often gets choked with snow as he never stops smiling while he cuts through the powder. By far the best skier here this week is Fred Racansky, another working guest, who began to ski at the age of 21. That was only 3 years ago! Fred skis over 100 days out of the season, is largely self-taught and would like one day to be a guide for Canadian Mountain Holidays. He likes to tour the outback with his skis, searching for new downhill terrain, camping out in the Columbia Icefields in snow caves and igloos, with candles and down sleeping gear for warmth. Fred works as a ski mechanic in Banff. He can turn them both ways!

Two skiers from Japan were at the Bugaboo Lodge this week, doing a story for some Japanese magazine. Hoso must have snapped over a thousand slides, while his assistant Aki took many notes.

I have saved Shirley Bridges for last as she is truly the most extraordinary member of our ski group at the Bugaboos

(Above) I like to use a lot of "anticipation" when I ski powder. Note my outside fist punching against the turn. When my movement is blocked, my lower body will uncoil and follow this lead.

(Left) Bill Pitt is an excellent powder skier. His form here, as he "anticipates" is flawless.

Lodge this week. Without revealing too much of her personal life, she has given me permission to mention that she is over 50 and is the wife of a prominent oil and gas executive. Another "world resident" most of Shirley's year is spent traveling, but not content with the tourist syndrome, Shirley prefers to live for a while in the areas which she visits. Moreover, she experiences life in those places much in the manner of the natives and is not reluctant to try any new adventure which demands courage and a good deal of stamina. She has a special interest in climbing expeditions and has scaled majestic peaks all over the world. Recently she has spearheaded a drive to enlist a helicopter rescue service for Andean mountain climbers. The local army has the choppers and what is needed is radio service, cooperation and a bit of empathy. Shirley has also been knocking on the door of Tom Bata (Bata Shoes) to come to the aid of Peruvian porters who badly need climbing boots. *She began to ski at the age of 39* and to mountain climb at 41! Shirley celebrated her fiftieth birthday scaling the high Cathedral Spire at Yosemite. Needless to say, she is in fantastic shape and somehow has managed to weave a broad range of intelligence into her physically active life-style. While many men feel a bit intimidated by such a vivacious *performer*, especially when they realize that Shirley's interests involve her more deeply than the frivolities of a dilettante, they are soon captivated by her curiously delicate grace and sensitivity. It was Shirley who scouted the woods that surround the Bugaboo Lodge until she found a spray of pussy willows to decorate its living room and Shirley who entertained us all one evening by dancing a native dance while balancing a glass of water on her forehead. As a skier she is

confident, strong and courageous. She does not hesitate on any run, and, while she blushes with embarassment at the stemming of her outside ski in tough conditions, I can verify that her descent is always rhythmic and graceful. I have never seen Shirley fall, and I found her perseverance and success against the usual hazards like steepness, breakable crust, old heavy snow and skiing through close pines positively aggravating, since the rest of us were all having problems! The itinerary for Mrs. Bridges' summer includes travel to Switzerland, Ontario and Alberta, Canada, hiking through British Columbia's wilderness, Berkeley, California, Houston, Texas, Mexico and Peru. I get out of breath just hearing about it! She has been a delightful addition to this group.

There were others, to whom I apologize for not having the space to include, but these brief sketches should give you some idea of whom you might find when you decide to try this marvelous adventure. Do it now. There are cornices, cliffs, couloirs, glaciers and pine textured moraines that await you, with names like Air Born, Groovy, Pyramid, Dome, Frenchman, Powder Pig, Black Forest, Evelyn's Crevasse, plus many that I can't mention. Least crowded and least expensive are the months of December and late April, when snow conditions vary from deep and steep to corn. I like April for sunshine and enjoy the challenge of variable snow conditions. Any month in the Bugaboos is a piece of heaven. This is no commercial hype. It is an honest appraisal from one very much like yourself who happens to love skiing with limited restrictions. In the Bugaboos, you will find the toughest, most beautiful skiing in the world. At the Bugaboo Lodge you will find the toughest, most beautiful people.

Chapter 5

TEACHING YOUR CHILD TO SKI

MANY OF THE LATEST changes in ski school curriculum are designed with chauvinistic motivation toward the formulation of a unique nationalistic system. Too often the changes are not introduced with the amelioration of the skier's learning process in mind, but are examples of innovation for the sake of innovation. "Let's call it a *wedge* this year; *snowplow* sounds too old fashioned . . ." "*Avalement* works, but let's call it *compression,* so as not to admit to European influence . . ." "Let's not mention angulation this year; it's too Austrian . . ." In most cases these semantic omissions in the descriptions of basic effective form are harmless and tolerable, but a great deal of pressure for *innovation* is placed upon ski educators who want their voice to be heard and accepted with credibility, in an era where innovation has come to be equated with *quality*. Admittedly, I have tried to stay in touch with all changes despite their national origin, in order to present for my readers an eclectic approach, but you can rest assured that if I introduce anything *new* to my readers, it will be because it is either more economical, more efficient or more graceful, and it will most definitely *not* be just for the sake of introducing something new, nor will it be to identify the technique as distinctively *mine*. Thus, the instruction offered here is little changed from the instructional methods presented in my previous skiing books. There has been no dramatic new development in ski technique. Commendably, many ski schools have come to recognize skiing as a head sport before being a physical one, and the trade magazines have been full of articles supporting that contention with such psychologically motivating titles as "Inner Skiing," etc.

In the area of ski education for children, I have noticed little change in ski school approaches for over two decades. While ski schools have recognized the need for more individualized intellectual methods among adult classes, few have begun to respect the special needs of the younger set. Still commonly seen on every beginner to novice slope is the stone faced female instructress, bored and unhappy with her job because she would rather be teaching adults on the more challenging side of the mountain, snowplowing her way down with a wake of 12 to 15 little ones plodding their way behind her, all in the same awkward joint stressing wedge position. Invariably, 90 percent of the children are sitting way back with their boots far in front, and the look on their faces suggests wonder at why adults bother with a frightening uncomfortable sport. Especially distressing to me is the tot who pushes off at the top of

his slope in this aberration of effective skiing form and tears straight down depending upon a leveling of the grade at the bottom to slow himself down! You know. I am sure you have seen them.

I believe that the wedge position is a criminal form of child abuse that should be outlawed. It is bad enough that schools teach it to adults. There are many adults who are in such poor physical condition that the triangular snowplow posture offers a false sense of security. If a ski student is wider at the waist than at the chest or shoulders, the antiquated posture might even be preferred, but for any reasonably athletic adult build and certainly for most children whose bodies are not yet distorted, the wedge manner of learning is contraindicated. I have had phenomenal success with the strictly parallel approach in the ski education of children. The ski instruction which follows is the report of my own daughter's first week. Cami, who is now 8, can carve her way down any slope with confidence and safety. Just last week, we stood together with the front of our skis hanging precariously over the lip of the mogul field below 8700-foot Emigrant Peak at Squaw Valley. While I studied the challenge with apprehension, searching for an easy line down, Cami looked up and said, "C'mon Dad, let's go . . . ," and with that she plunged over the lip laughing and hooping as she attacked each bump and sprayed aggressive walls of snow with each edge set! I shook my head with amazement, as my little snowbird has only about 50 days of total skiing experience behind her! Parallel, from the beginning. Moreover, she can describe the basic mechanics of a turn verbally, so I know her awareness is total and not merely imitative. I can tell you that in teaching Cami the parallel technique, I have avoided a great burden of fear which I feel for other children when I see them descending an irregular run in the wedge position. Should Cami fall, I know it won't be with one ski pointed directly across the other. I can think of no more dangerous way to ski than with the "wedge" or "snowplow." It was never intended to be a way to ski. The snowplow position developed as a teaching device to explain *angulation* and edging with the body weight pressed against the outside ski. Children are so close to their skis that parallel movements are easy for them to master and angulation can be taught when traversing. To contort their little bodies into wedge positions just because we learned to ski that way when we were adults is to do them a great injustice. It is worse than that. It is child abuse!

SKI INSTRUCTION FOR YOUR CHILD

ALTHOUGH YOU HAVE read it in countless articles with similar titles, it is worth repeating that no child should be forced to participate in skiing or *any* activity, be it physical or mental. That would be the surest way to turn off a child and possibly give him a psychological scar which can have just the opposite effect than the one you intended by the coercion. On the other hand, it is your natural obligation, as an influential parent to *expose* your child to a variety of forms for creative expression. My dad used to say, "You can lead a horse to water, but you can't make him drink." The cliché has many applications. As skiers, you understandably want your offspring to enjoy skiing, in order to have a sport in which your entire family can participate for many years. Just don't rush it; and, when the child gets his first taste, don't choke him with an excess of the sport, or you may kindle a rejection that is as intense as your obsession.

Pre-school children who have not been mother-smothered will be attracted to any physical activity that is a form of *play;* particularly when other children are engaged in the same sport. This fact suggests two prerequisites for a successful introduction of your child to skiing. First, make it seem like play, and secondly, let him see other children his age playing the same "game."

Of course, if you have never stripped yourself of the plastic adult veneer and entered your child's world in other forms of play, don't expect him to suddenly accept you as a playmate on the slope. It takes months, years in some cases, of honest participation in his unpretentious world of make-believe, before a child will accept you as a friend with whom it is worth playing. We all want to take pride in our children. We are pleased when they are well-mannered in public, when they eat as fast and as thoroughly as we do, when they learn their arithmetic and spell well. We are so anxious for them to behave like adults that we frequently create little adult-like freaks who have been so brainwashed with adult rules of propriety, they have missed precious experiences of youth for which they will never again have the opportunity. Time passes quickly, and youth is so much more precious because of time's fleetingness. Enjoy the 3-year-old behavior of your 3-year-old, for soon she will be 4 and no longer interested in the things that are important to a child of 3. If your 4-year-old would rather be making a snowman or catching snowflakes in her mouth than sliding down a hill on skis, don't bury your head in your pillow and cry. That very same child could one day be a Marielle Goitschel, but her maturational level for interest in skiing may come at the age of five.

There is, in fact, no proper age to begin skiing. A fear-indoctrinated child may never overcome the phobias planted in her mind by overprotective parents who have not exposed her to activities wherein she might have chalked up

Fig. 5-2: Teach her a good traversing posture, and she'll never catch a downhill edge when she turns!

a few physical accomplishments, be they as slight as one or two good turns on skis. Some Olympic champions were strapped into the boards at the age of 2. Stein Eriksen. Jean-Claude Killy. Karli Schranz traced his first exposure back to the age of 3. Any of you who, like myself, did not begin to ski until mid-twenties, must have muttered to yourself more than once, "I wish I had started at that age . . . ." every time some grade school schussboomer sprayed snow in your face. Well, we can't turn back the clock, but neither should we be so anxious to turn that clock ahead. Be honest with yourself. Is the reason why you want your child to be a precocious champion really because you feel it will benefit him; or is it to fatten your own ego?

It has been my experience after 15 years of teaching the sport, that children in this country are seldom ready for any scientific understanding of the physics of a turn before the age of 12. Few are ready for ski school type of instruction before the age of 7, and even fewer will accept the discomfort of the most basic beginning exercises before the age of 4. What we do find at the 4-year-old level is a surprising capacity for imitation, an insatiable love for play, and little feet whose toes get cold very fast. That imitative capacity can be capitalized upon. Look at the photo of my 4-year-old daughter Cameron following me in a traverse. (Fig. 5-2) She may not understand why her downhill shoulder should be the same slant as the slope but she has startled other skiers by shouting down to them from the chairlift, "Drop your downhill shoulder!" a phrase she hears from me so often. No less astounding is her conversation at the dinner table when tales of how "Daddy and me jumped over the whole mountain" are mixed with recapitulations of how she kept her "knees bent," her "skis together" and her "poles behind her." Is there any reader over 40 who will not admit to the value of rote or imitative learning? As I write this text, Cameron has turned 5. The coming season will be only her second winter exposure to skiing. Her first season was brief, about four weekends. You may be interested in reading what we accomplished along with a few suggestions for starting your own little one on skis.

We waited for a sunny initiation. I think this is important. You will have problems enough maintaining your child's attention without having to wipe her tears over cold feet! During the long drive from Westport, Connecticut, to my chalet on Glen Ellen in Vermont, we sang a slew of songs from "Twinkle, Twinkle, Little Star" to "One Plump Robin," and when we had replayed all the songs she had learned in nursery school about ten times, we made up a few of our own. To the tune of "Swing Low, Sweet Chariot," we sang "Ski Slow, Oh, Ski Patrol," which began an enlightening conversation between us about the Ski Patrol and its function. Children like to feel protected. Cami seemed a little more secure when she learned that she would not only have her Daddy near to protect her on the slope, but even the Ski Patrol. With two Popsicle sticks, which we had to strip of their ice-cream, of course, I explained how some skiers cross their skis and fall. Keeping the sticks parallel I emphasized that she could never get hurt if both of her skis were pointed in the same direction. It wasn't long before Cameron had the sticks in hand, schussing down my chest and over my knee as my wife kept her eyes on the road. Establishing a bit of meaningful imagery is an important part of the early indoctrinational experience. Try to find a toy skier. If you can't, buy a couple of Popsicles. Drive to your ski area the night before a bright sunny day. Have a good breakfast and don't rush off to the slope. Start her on skis during the warmest part of the day, about 11 AM. and plan to quit before 3. What can you do before 11? Cami and I built a snowlady with a neat carrot nose, ". . . so someone can watch the house while we go skiing . . ."

On the morning of the first day, please check the outdoor thermometer in the shade and dress your child accordingly. From the top down, make sure she has a warm hat, one that will stay down over her ears. The strap of her gogles can secure it. By all means, invest in a pair of goggles; they will protect her eyes from the direct and reflected light of the sun, and they will make her feel very professional. A long scarf will insulate the vital area of her throat and give added heat to her lungs. Get a colorful one; kids love bright things. Long underwear for children is tough to find. It is important enough for you to at least spend some time at a sewing machine recycling your husband's old longjohns; the ones that have the big tear in the crotch. You could probably make your child's bottoms out of one adult size leg. Remember that children have little tolerance for discomfort. Keep your child warm and you will have half the battle won! Make sure that you dress *together*. She will appreciate wearing the same outfit as the "big people." Silk or nylon stockings under a long pair of wool stockings is next; short socks tend to slip under the child's heels after a few runs. No holes in the stockings, please. The turtleneck shirt is here to stay. Try to find one in her size or sew a turtleneck onto one of her T-shirts. Get a neat sweater. Something with Santa's reindeer on it or snowflakes; something warm but colorful, with a crew or turtleneck. The outer skin can be a snowsuit but NOT WOOL. Snow sticks to wool and your child will

Fig. 5-3: The Jacobs Corporation, 5735 Arapahoe Ave. in Boulder, Colorado, has a fantastic line of children's clothing. They call it Hot Gear. Cami's outfit is not only cute; it's warm and comfortable.

soon be refrigerated if anything wool is on the exterior. Gloves are so important. Mittens, of course, are warmest. Get them with gauntlets and they won't fill with snow. Don't buy cheap mittens; it would not take much to freeze those tiny fingers. Fur inside is great; leather or vinyl outside. I think it is criminal the way some parents send their children out in the snow with wool gloves that soon become a cake of ice. Invariably, the same parents wear wool socks outside their ski pants. So much for clothing. (Fig. 5-3)

Boots are a separate problem. For years, children were the poorest equipped in this department, but during the past 5 or 6 years, manufacturers have been recognizing the need. It puzzles me why the more popular companies have taken the longest to provide something substantial for our little ones. Surely it is profitable; a child could outgrow her boots annually. While this should increase sales and lock in a steady customer for the dealers, it also puts a nasty dent in the consumer's pocket book. One way to get around this is to find a friendly neighbor whose child is a year older than yours. If they don't ski, lure them to the slopes for a weekend. They'll get hooked, buy their kid an outfit more expensive than the one you bought for your prodigy, and be stuck with his boots when he outgrows them in a year. You, of course, will then be quite happy to help out a neighbor and take the boots off his hands for a token figure (no more than half the original price). Children are not as hard on boots as we are; in a year, those boots will be almost like new, but better (they'll be broken in)! Another suggestion to beat the expanding size problem is to have junior try on his new boots in his sneakers; let him ski a whole season wearing his sneakers inside his boots and his boots should be just the right size next year, or perhaps a year later.

Fig. 5-4: Cami's *gators* keep the snow out and the warmth in!
Fig. 5-5: Mine are neat, too!

Fig. 5-6: Have her walk in your steps.

Fig. 5-7: "Making steps" in the snow is a great way to teach *edging*.

If his boots are not high enough to prevent snow from entering, sew up a pair of "gators" with some warm material and Velcro. Wrap it around his ankle well below the boot top and almost to his knee. Marge made a pair for Cami out of rabbit skin. (Fig. 5-4) I liked them so much that I asked for a pair for myself. Gators are a must in deep snow. (Fig. 5-5)

Off to the slope. From the chalet it is only about 300 feet to the novice area lift. The uphill walk is breathtaking, but it is a perfect warmup exercise. Kids need to "warm up" just as grownups should. Driving right to the door of the ticket booth, hopping on the lift and skiing before the body is even awake is a slothful, dangerous practice of too many skiers. You would be a lot kinder to your body if you deliberately parked your car as far away from that ticket booth as you are permitted. Walk with a brisk pace and drink up some of the clean air you have missed in the city. Your circulation will then be ready for the demands of rigorous skiing, and your joints will be well oiled. An Austrian friend of mine used to warm up his ski class for 5 minutes before every morning's session on the hill. Hartwig had his students shout cadence as they performed the exercises he prescribed. Throughout the vast acreage of Sugarbush Valley you could hear the group every morning chanting "Ski! Heil!" until some idiot with a Nazi fixation complained to the Corporation and had it stopped. Your child can't be expected to understand the value of pre-ski exercise. You, as a more enlightened parent must lead the way. The exercise may be simply a walk. The cadence can be a game of counting. (Why not train her mind along with her body?) On the way to the ticket office, point out things of visual interest. Train her to see. How many adults do you know who live their lives as if they were wearing a plow horse's blinders? Ask her how big the man was who made those tracks in the new snow. Discover a cumulus cloud and watch it boil upwards. How many New York license plates can she count in the parking lot? Show her how to carry her skis "like a big girl." At 4, she should be able to carry her own skis, if they are not taller than she is, and they *should* be no taller!

Put your own skis on first. Children get impatient fast, and you are challenging a most limited attention span if you ask her to wait for you after she has been snapped into her bindings. If you can't bend low enough to help her when you are on skis, you are in pretty bad shape and have no business skiing, let alone teaching someone else, especially a child—place her in the qualified hands of a good ski school, and find yourself an abdominal board.

You must learn how to go up, before you can come down. Cameron liked to herringbone behind me (Fig. 5-6), but soon we concentrated on the sidestep. In a traverse direction I explained to her the important principle of keeping her shoulders the same slant as the hill. I believe this little axiom to be one of the most important balance factors in the sport of skiing, so why not let it be the first thing learned. As your child's instructor, you will be doing a lot of repeating. Deliberately repeat the salient rules and you will condition your student's reflexes to act appropriately. The sidestep climbing posture is the proper traverse position. With Cami, it wasn't even too early to explain that the uphill ski should be a little bit ahead, as we proceeded to "make steps" in the snow. A child of 4 has a pretty good idea of what steps look like. By "making steps" in the snow, she was learning how to edge surreptitiously. (Fig. 5-7) The full comprehension of

Fig. 5-8: Cami's first run downhill. Her knees were too straight. She did better when I told her to try to *kneel* on her ski tips.

Fig. 5-9: A crouch will get her center of gravity closer to her skis and improve her balance.

Fig. 5-10: *Before* she falls, *you* fall, to show her that *everyone* falls, occasionally.

edge probably comes at a later age, but a simple demonstration was all that was necessary, in the case of my daughter, to show how a flat ski slides downhill while a ski that "makes steps" will not. We climbed with the sidestep in both directions, rewarding ourselves with a downhill run in between each climb. I chose a hill that went uphill again after the flat runout, in order to have her stop automatically.

The best downhill running position for children is the posture favored by many modern adult skiers whose alma mater is the school of squat. With her skis apart about hip width, Cami assumed the constipated position and pushed off with her right ski pole while her left hand held mine. One difficulty with skiing hand-in-hand is that an adult's skis will, of course, be faster. The solution is to keep your own skis in a wedge position to check your speed. It is my considered opinion, however, that the "snowplow" or wedge maneuver should *not* be taught to a child of 4 during the initial learning period, or it will become a crutch that the child will cling to tenaciously for many years. From the beginning I have instilled the awareness in my daughter that the safest way to ski is with the skis pointed in the same direction. As close to the ground as pre-school children are, there is really little need for the snowplow maneuvers. Believe that, and you won't have your heart in your mouth every time you see your little one schussing a hill with one ski pointed across the path of the other; there is no more dangerous position. While the wedge has its place (for checking speed) it should be taught at a later time, certainly after the child has made a few parallel turns. Gradually encourage your child to stand a bit taller as her downhill runs improve. We should try to save the low position for unweighting in the turns. (Fig. 5-8 and Fig. 5-9)

You may be surprised to read that "Falling" is the title of the next step in the child's learning process. It is followed, of course, by instruction for "Getting Up." Every skier falls. Some psychologists analyze our motivation for skiing as a conquest of a castration fixation—where we push ourselves to the brink of total destruction and suddenly save ourselves with a controlled turn. More often than not, we miss that saving turn and wipe out. Since falls are so common and perhaps even inevitable, learning to fall properly should be an early lesson. By falling deliberately, a thing of fear can be transformed into a kind of fun. Whether you call it a derriere, a backside, a bottom or a heinie, that round thing behind you is the most padding you have got to cushion a fall. "Watch me, Cami. I'm going to ski down and slide on my heinie . . ." I called out to my daughter as I pushed off. It is important to swing your seat to the side before you hit. Do it, and your kid will think it's pretty funny. Funny enough to try it herself, laughing all the way. (Fig. 5-10) Be sure to caution her about not trying to stop her fall with her poles!

Getting up after a fall may present some problems. Show your child the customary method illustrated in Chapter 3 but keep in mind that his little arms have not got the power of yours. If he falls on flat ground, it may be very difficult for him to rise. Most of the time I help my daughter. She will be more capable of pulling herself up next season. If your child hasn't been deprived of other self-sufficient activities to motivate independence, she will actually look forward to the day when she can rise by herself. Every time I offered to help Cameron last season she was quite adamant about my letting her do it herself, and only after four or five desperate

Fig. 5-11 (left): Three hands are better than two. At Glen Ellen the lift attendants are courteous and helpful.

Fig. 5-12 (right): Take her for a few runs like this. Give her a lot of *mileage.*

attempts did she look up and offer me her hand. If the fall takes place on a slope, gravity will assist your child. Whenever he does rise by himself, make a big fuss about it and slip him a reward.

Pavlovian as it may sound, the old reward-for-good—and-punishment-for-bad trick still is a sound system of child training, skiing not withstanding. Knowledgeable parents today have replaced the sugar reward with a chewable vitamin C tablet or fruit and nuts. The razor strap beating that conditioned many of us through our recalcitrant childhoods may have been moderated considerably, but the basic fact of a child's give-nothing-for-no-return attitude is understood by the least of armchair psychologists. If a short downhill run in good form is rewarded while a run with stiff knees or skis too wide apart brings nothing but an admonishment and another tiring climb up the hill, your child will learn her first day's lesson fast.

Sporadically, during her first day's exposure, I took Cami on the chairlift and skied down holding her between my legs. This is a most important part of your child's initial exposure in the struggle for self-sufficiency.

My wife took Cami's poles and mine after my daughter and I slid over to the lift. Riding the chairlift was one of the "rewards" I promised for good skiing. All children will be initially apprehensive about boarding the lift. Most children love to ride the swings at the local playground, though. Why not draw an analogy between the two? The idea of riding a swing together with one of her parents should appeal to any well-adjusted child. If yours is one of those blessed little creatures I have seen who scream up a tantrum at the least suggestion of trying something daring or new, don't push the child. *Forcing* him to ride the chair would be a serious mistake. Just say, "OK, Junior, you don't have to ride up. We will just keep climbing." His hedonistic instinct which seems to be a part of normal human nature will soon move him to ask *you* if, next time, you could both ride the lift.

On the way to the launching pad relieve some of the child's anxiety by taking her mind off the approaching challenge. I held Cami's hand and we both counted the number of sliding steps from our practice area to the chairlift. I shouted the even numbers and she followed with the odds. If your child can't count past ten, think up some other diversion, and spend a little more time teaching her how to count when you get home.

At the loading spot, hold your child firmly as you both observe at least three sets of skiers board the chair and take off. If you are lucky, one of those skiers will be just a few years older than your little one. Another strange characteristic about human nature is the drive to compete, particularly in boys, who have had to lead the pack or get trampled ever since they were sperms. Rest assured, if another child rides before you, your Junior will be *anxious* to have the experience. My Cami may be only part sperm, but she is as competitive as any boy her age, so my job was easy. Slide into the takeoff track immediately after the chair in front of yours disembarks. We did it holding hands. Be sure to place your child on the same side of the track as the lift attendant. He may have to assist you when you board. You should have plenty of time to plan your next movements before your chair comes up behind you. With a firm grip under each of Junior's armpits turn to the approaching lift and get ready to lift him as you sit. Lift and slide him as far back into the seat as you can, while you sit. The lift attendant will know enough to tilt the chair back a bit so you don't get hit in the hamstrings with the seat. Tucked far back in the chair, your child's skis should now be erect, his legs almost straight. With one arm across his chest, reach up with the other and pull down the foot rest and safety bar. You're off. Please remember to say "Wheeeeeee!" or "Yahooooo!" or something to color the experience as *fun.* (Fig. 5-11)

Don't waste the ride up. It is a great opportunity to point out errors, laugh at funny falls, cheer other children skiers who seem to have it all together, and catch some snowflakes in your mouth. If is it sunny and warm, open Junior's zipper a little and loosen his scarf. Sing a few songs with him and do all you can to help him relax and enjoy the ride up. Well before the unloading platform, point to the sign that says "Approaching Unloading Platform. Raise Safety Bar." The sign should also say "Raise Your Ski Tips." Discuss its meaning with the child. Restore his confidence by telling him you will be holding him as you descend, and that the slide down the unloading hill will be just like his downhill runs on the bottom. Also instruct that when you say "Stand," he should stand up and let the skis slide. There it is. "*Stand!*" and don't be afraid to raise your voice a few decibels.

Descending from the unloading spot for the first time, I held Cami much the same as when I loaded her, pushed off with parallel skis next to hers and gradually stemmed my outside ski, gently pushing her skis into the turn at the bottom. We made it! If you do, take a moment to look back with your child, to watch other skiers descend. If some klutz should dump and get tied up like a pretzel, explain to your future skier that the demise occurred because Ms. Klutz was sitting back too far, or bending too much at the waist, or whatever. Reassure Junior that he will never fall getting off a lift because he *knows* how to ski downhill! Then slip him another C tab.

For our first day's downhill runs, I assumed a wedged position and placed Cami between my legs with my hands on her shoulders. This allowed her to ski parallel and get the thrill of skiing at a fast but controlled pace. (Fig. 5-12) Each time we traversed I mentioned the change in the slant of the

Fig. 5-13 (left): Don't waste her mileage time. Talk about "making steps," keeping her shoulders "just like the hill," etc.
Fig. 5-14 (right): If she dangles, her mileage with you will be worthless. Don't allow it!

hill, and we adjusted our shoulders accordingly. Simultaneously I recalled the ski angle for "making steps" in the snow, and Cameron began to traverse in pretty good form. We kept our traverses long, turning at the sides of the slope to temper our speed. As we approached each turning point I told Cami to sink down, applying pressure to her shoulders. This gave her skis a momentary weight release which I tried to time with my directions to "Point your skis to the *other* woods." Traversing most novice runs, there are woods in front of your skis and woods behind your skis. The word *traverse* is a bit pedantic when speaking to some 4-year-olds. Most of them know what *woods* mean, though. Try to keep your instructions within your child's vocabulary of understanding. (Fig. 5-13)

Some of you who read this may take issue with the simplicity of my directions for a parallel turn in the last paragraph. If you, like many, have spent years trying to perfect your own parallel turn, you might even take offense with my audacious insinuation that a weight release and reversed pointing of the skis is all that's necessary. Well, not *all;* remember the other axiom: "slant the shoulders the same as the hill and traverse on your uphill edges." Truthfully, that simplification is the basis of a successful parallel turn, but it especially works when the skier's height is only about a yard (and particularly when she is skiing between the legs of an advanced skier who holds on tenaciously to her shoulders). If you try to imitate the posture I have recommended when skiing with your child, be certain to hold a strongly edged lower ski in the traverses. A simple rise upward and a little back in the wedge position will effect a movement of your ski tips toward the fall line. Sink down as you direct the child to do the same and weight your outside ski as you tell her to point her skis ". . . toward the other woods." Another device that is effective is to have her point her inside finger, (the finger that is *inside* the intended turn) to the new direction along with you, just as she begins to twist her skis. This will require a kind of anticipatory movement of her upper body which will soon be followed by her lower body and her skis.

If everything is working well, and you think she can handle one more detail (it is wise not to give your child too many *rules* all at once; let her master one thing at a

time), do mention that "everything uphill is ahead, the uphill ski, the uphill knee, hip and shoulder all lead us to the woods . . ." My Cameron had no difficulty with this perception, although I had to pad it with a little imagery: "Finish every turn with a *bow* to your downhill audience, Cami. Look downhill . . ." I said as we began a new traverse, "See Marge. She is our audience. Bow to her. That's it. OK. Here comes another turn. Sink DOWN and point your skis to the other woods. Neat. Now, look at Marge and BOW. GOOD TURN. Wheeeee!" She giggled all the way down and I slipped her a few raisins.

Moguls create problems, for you, not for the child between your legs. She has her skis together and can easily turn on the top of a bump if necessary, but your skis are in snowplow position. Your reflexes had better be quick. Your edging had better be positive. Even if you avoid turning in the mogul section (and you certainly *should* on the child's first day), traversing several bumps in that wedge position can be pretty tricky—particulary if the terrain is fast. My suggestion is to try to avoid the challenge, unless you are a strong and very experienced skier. If it is unavoidable, traverse the mogul field edging your downhill ski sharply and make your turn at the very edge of the slope. Above all, don't reveal any apprehension you might have to your little one. She must feel that you are the best skier in the world and fully capable of saving her should an emergency arise.

When you are 25-50 feet away from the bottom, let her try a schuss, turning by herself on the flat. She may surprise you. Cameron made a neat parallel turn, turned and giggled, "Let's do it again, Dad!" Several runs with your child between your legs will condition her to speed and the kinetic uncertainty of sliding, which can be pretty disconcerting even to a beginning adult. Only when an individual feels a certain amount of control over the sliding movement of skis will he or she be encouraged to "do it again . . ." With a child, in the between your legs position I have recommended, you represent that control.

I should emphasize that you are to thwart any attempt by the child to simply hang from your arms and dangle her skis. (Fig. 5-14) Do your best to relate her movements to correct parallel form. You are, in effect, *conditioning her reflexes* and should continue to do so until she automatically sinks down to turn (unweighting), edges her skis in the traverse (resisting centrifugal force and gravity), and angles her shoulders the same slant as the hill (to oppose centripetal force and gravity). Be firm and tell her that the slope is a skiing place not a sleeping place. If you are not forceful on this point right from the beginning, you will end up with a heavy limp weight and straying skis which could easily hook under yours and cause you both to tumble.

The second day should be much like the first, except that your child will be much steadier on her feet and probably more courageous. The trips down from the chairlift should still be wrapped in the security blanket of your skis, but on the bottom you can begin to work on the child's self-determined turn. Climb, then have her schuss, and turn to the right. Then, climb again and

Fig. 5-15 (left): Her little legs will tire. Time to play Poma-Lift!

Fig. 5-16 (right): Cami traversing in good form.

have her try a turn to the left. If she tires of the climbing steps, use your pole and play Poma lift, as in Fig.5-15, but be sure to tuck that pole shaft snugly under her bottom and tell her not to *sit*. While you sidestep, her skis should be parallel and *sliding*. Advise her not to *step*.

Here is where my philosophy differs from the American Teaching Method. While the snow plow turn or wedge position is useful in emergency situations and should be learned at a later stage, I see no reason to teach it to a child who is much closer to the ground than we are and considerably lighter on the skis. If her skis are no longer than her height, she will easily perform a parallel turn, if you can just get her to coordinate the twist of her knees and feet with an unweighting motion (preferably a *down* motion). Demonstrate a straight run down a gradual decline, then turn as you sink down by bending your knees and pushing them toward the direction of your intention. If your little one is used to being coddled, she might play games with you and refuse to follow your directions, announcing her ploy with a statement like "I can't!" Don't accept it. If she gets away with that cop-out at the age of 4, you can bet she will resort to it all through her life. Convince her that she can do anything a big person can, if she just keeps *trying*. Offer her a prize for the effort, a prize for trying, but offer her a *bigger* prize if she *succeeds*. I did notice, with Cameron, that her turns were better and quicker when an obstacle was the primary motivating factor. Thus, in a wide open nearly flat area, she often just skied straight, until her skis automatically stopped because of a subtle rise in terrain. When the speed of one of those runs took her past the subtle rise and down another decline she headed straight for the woods, and I gulped when she whipped a beautiful christie just 6 inches from the edge.

The parallel turns pre-school children perform "automatically" are skidded turns, usually on the flat bottom portion of the skis. Instructors will be quick to point out that many adults turn their skis the same way. Much of

the GLM approach capitalizes upon this fact, and some schools actually applaud the uncontrolled skid turn as an effective maneuver. Well, it *is* a turn, and the beginner *does* leave his ski weekend thinking he has mastered the art of skiing. "So what, if he is confined to the flat beginner slope; at least he is outdoors doing something," many ski school directors will say, "He'll never be an athlete anyway. Look at that pot belly he's carrying around . . ."

The fact of the matter is that controlled skiing relies upon the ability to *carve* a turn, with properly edged skis. By all means, allow your child to continue his skidded turns in the early part of his learning process but bear in mind that those uncontrolled movements are *preliminary* and as soon as he is skidding when he wants to, to the right and to the left, it is time to modify his turns by introducing the proper method of edging. One of the reasons I believe in spending a good deal of time on the traverse maneuver is that it is essentially the beginning and end of every turn. A child (or beginning adult, for that matter), who has been traversing *in good form* for several days need only to be reminded of the form when he is halfway into his turn, and what was once skidded will become a *carved* turn. Don't be afraid to shout *"traverse,"* the moment your student is facing downhill, with the provision, of course, that he fully understands the meaning of the word and its preferred posture. The word *traverse* was not beyond the comprehension of my 4-year-old. Because of this importance of the traversing position, I encourage my students, young or old, to use the posture even when they *climb* with a sidestep! Points to remember about the traverse position are 1. Skis on their uphill edges, 2. Everything uphill should be slightly ahead (the uphill ski, boot, knee, hip and shoulder), 3. Tilt the shoulders to the same slant as the hill. The last point becomes

Fig. 5-17: Progress to hand-in-hand as soon as possible.

Fig. 5-18: Insist upon her good traversing posture (it's worth a few raisins) and slow your own speed with a wedge.

less imperative as the snow gets deeper, but is absolutely required for optimum balance on packed or hard terrain. (Fig. 5-16)

With the traverse reasonably under control, which should take 3 or 4 days, your child is ready to step out from in between your protective legs on all future downhill runs. I recommend the hand-in-hand method next, again, without poles. You must continue a wedged descent in order to keep up with Junior, but he is now fully capable of performing parallel turns, with your verbal directions and a sufficient amount of raisins in your pocket. From the top of the novice run, begin a traverse with your child above in good parallel form and you below in an edged snowplow position. Control your speed by releasing your edges, just enough to keep up with your student. You should be firmly grasping her downhill hand; verbally adjusting her traversing posture. As you approach the turning point near the edge of the woods, tell the child that you are both going to turn by rising UP (in preparation) and sinking DOWN to turn. Rising *up* in your wedged position will automatically cause your tips to drift downhill if you release your edge; her ski tips will follow the same gravitational pull. Shout "DOWN" at the turning point and weight your outside ski, edging it as you do so. Hand-in-hand, your child will whip around you. Remind her to point her skis to "the other woods" and slip in a TRAVERSE command. These turns, with the child on the *outside* of the turn will be easier. (Fig. 5-17)

With the child *inside* the turn while skiing hand-in-hand, you must guide her *outside ski by sliding your inside* ski right along side of it. If you fail to do this, her skis might run over your inside ski, and that could cause a tumble. At this precarious moment in the turn, I have found it effective to tell the child to look at the other woods." (Fig. 5-18) This will prompt her to twist her upper body in the direction of the turn, and the anticipatory movement will soon be followed by a twisting of her knees, feet and skis. Be sure to shout "DOWN" at the turning phase, to effect a weight release, and "TRAVERSE" when her skis point downhill, in order to get her skis back onto their uphill edges.

While your little one may be ready to solo on the first day, I must repeat: *don't push her.* Every child has his own individual hangups and courage level. Let him tell *you* when he is ready to solo. Most children will seek that independence shortly after their first successful turn while holding your hand. Treat the poles as a *reward* for turning properly without them ("only really good skiers use their poles"). Watch your child's face during his first solo run. Does he appear to be enjoying it? Is he laughing? (Fig. 5-19) If his look is sour or frightened, he needs more training hand-in-hand. And, more raisins. Point to other children on the slope. He must not feel that he is the only little one in a grown-up world. It has got to become the child's world. You must become the intruder. And you will, soon enough. In a year or two, he will begin to wonder why *old people* ski at all, since it is obviously so much *fun*! You will have a new problem, then: trying to convince him that it can be a family sport; and, the more he improves, the harder you will have to work at keeping *yourself* in shape!

After a few solos, set up a mini-slalom course with your ski poles. Let her *watch* as *you* make a few runs through the course. Tell her that *someday* she will be able to do the same, and maybe *win a medal*! But stall her first encounter. This is the *teasing method* of child

Fig. 5-19: Her first solo will give you goose-bumps.

Fig. 5-20 (above): Upright between the turns, have her *crouch down* to turn. The drop will effect a weight release and make her axial motion easier.

Fig. 5-21 (left): Your goal is to get her to *carve* her turns on the inside edges. Tell her to show you the *bottoms* of her skis, on every turn!

Fig. 5-22 (below): Pavlov was right!

89

Fig. 5-23: Kids don't want to hear about ski technique. They want to have fun. Games are motivational. Slip in the instruction and physical training surreptitiously. Here, I'm developing the young thigh muscles of Tracy and Blair. I would hardly get as pleasant a response if I asked them to do deep knee bends!

motivation. It really works. He will soon be begging to try "the gates." After a couple of days of "You are not ready, yet," concede. But tell him that the medal is for skiing through *four* gates (borrow your wife's poles). Then, let him practice with two. Successful turns must be praised and rewarded. Poor form should be received with just a negative nod of your head and another demonstration by you, or your wife, or both of you. Every so often, flash the medal and shine it up.

While you are evaluating her form and demonstrating, be sure to emphasize a more erect posture *between* the turns, and a flexed posture *during* the turns. (Fig. 5-20) With her center of gravity closer to her skis, Cami's turns were effortless. I cheated a little by filling the groove down the center of her skis with hot wax. That groove is only important when a child starts jumping. You may consider yourself a success when you see your junior racer turning on *the edges* of his skis. (Fig. 5-21) Then, you will realize that all the proper traverse form practice conditioned his reflexes to oppose centrifugal force, and you won't have to worry about him catching a downhill edge! The moment you see space under his downhill edges, sigh a breath of relief, and give *yourself* a few raisins. You are both to be congratulated! Keep stoking your child with praise and rewards, and by all means try to enlist some other child to play in the same "game." A medal after a week's good effort and four successfully negotiated gates will be welcomed in awe! (Fig. 5-22)

Tears can be a sign of fatigue (if it is late in the day) or frustration at not being able to please you. Don't make it seem that important. Invent little games. Younger children will respond even more readily to games on skis, and if you are clever, you can relate the move-

ments required for the "game" to actual skiing mechanics. Whether the tears are sincere or mere ploys to test your response, *games* will effectively turn off the water. (Fig. 5-23)

Fatigue is an adversary that you should recognize and combat. There are two effective weapons, rest and nourishment. As I mentioned in a previous paragraph, don't *push* your child. You can probably use frequent rests yourself, so don't feel timid about making more than one visit to the ski lodge for some hot soup or an orange. On the other hand, don't underestimate the strength of your little one. My Cami, now 5, climbed the Burrows trail with me yesterday to the very top of Camel's Hump, a peak about 2.9 miles from the start of the trail, east of Huntington Center, Vermont. The Long Trail guidebook estimated the climbing time at 2¾ hours. We did it in 2½ hours with three rest stops. Today, I have sore knees, while Cameron is buzzing around like a roadrunner.

This chapter should give you enough guidance to get your child off to a good start. Cami is at the disadvantage of having divorced parents; consequently, she is only with me for about three weekends a ski season. If you can begin your Junior with at least one, full week, there will be great value in the continuity of the experience. If you are fortunate to have him on skis for one whole season, he will probably be skiing rings around you by next spring. One final word of caution: don't attempt to teach *anyone* unless you are in top physical condition and have a clear understanding of basic ski technique. If you don't qualify, put your little one in the hands of a qualified ski instructor, but first be sure he loves kids and has a few raisins in his pocket.

Pavlov was right! Cami's reward for good skiing this year is a pair of Garmont racing boots.

Chapter 6

THE GRAND SKI TOUR

Does it beat schlepping for yourself?
Is it worth the price?
Can it satisfy any level skier?

The author cutting a neat turn down a steep slope.

OF COURSE THE ANSWERS to our opening questions must depend upon the quality of the ski tour. It doesn't have to cost a grand, but you had better figure on it costing at least half a grand for a memorable week if you live far from ski country. As with any luxury expenditure you can expect to get what you pay for. Low budget skiers have no right to expect plush accommodations in exchange for modest investments. For this brief report, we chose a tour that provides what we feel is an ideal return for just a little more than modest cost. Our country is laced with many tours of its type in every major city. Since schlepping for yourself is the first alternative challenge, we selected a tour company that is as far away from skiing as you can get in these 50 states. David Travels operates out of North Miami, Florida. That's a long schlepp!

David Travels is a young agency more accustomed to arranging tours which bring travelers to Miami at the lowest fares imaginable (can you believe, under $50 from New York City to Miami?) and junket gamblers from all over the east coast to Las Vegas. In exchange for the adventure, I have been hired by David Travels to give some private lessons. This ski tour is a new venture which David Travels president, Louis Robinson, has advised us, will be a test run to evaluate the investment and the return against the adventure. Marge and I are loners who have always appreciated the freedom of arranging our own ski trips, so we approach this experience with the same skepticism, I imagine, with which many readers might respond to the concept of traveling with a large group. So far, we have been pleasantly surprised. There have been no hassles. No intolerable regimentation. No threat to our free nature.

At Kennedy Airport, we boarded a Trans International Airways DC-10 laden with furs, cameras, and ski paraphernalia along with a few hundred other Miami-bound travelers who were south bound for quite different reasons. Most of them were elderly, conforming to the stereotype of the typical Miami Beach bound tourist, winter clothed and pallored, and looking forward, I am sure, to the warm comforting rays of the tropical sun. We took off about an hour later than scheduled when only one bus driver showed up to transport us to the plane. TIA apparently does not load at the customary "gate" (which is probably why the cost of flying with this airline is so much less), so two buses are used to transfer passengers from the gate to the aircraft. There was the usual grumbling among some of the less seasoned travelers who were intolerant of the absent driver's illness. The flight was quite pleasant, and the

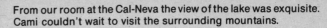
seats were comfortable. By the time we had just lost the taste of the continental breakfast which was served, we were already approaching the sunshine state of Florida. Warm tropical winds caressed and bent the palms gracefully and we felt absurd in our winter clothes as we stepped down the gangplank into summer in February. A Red Cap limousine managed to haul our skis, luggage and us to a friend's home for a very reasonable fee.

We had arranged to spend a few days in Cocoanut Grove before joining the David Travels ski group. We enjoyed eating at the Oak Feed health food restaurant in the Grove, and it is just a hop, skip and a jump from the beach at Key Biscayne which has become one of our favorite running and sunning areas. In interesting contrast to the elderly predominant Miami Beach population, the Grove teems with young people, attractive girls in tight jeans and see-through blouses, suntanned joggers and bicyclists, pseudo and legit artists with magnificent beards and an obviously gay contingent, quietly doing their own thing. Curiously, even the dopers passing their joints around on the street corners looked tan but characteristically round shouldered and undernourished. We reserved a couple of hours out of each day for some weight resistance exercise at Dalia Valle's gymnasium on 8th and Washington Streets in Miami Beach, and together with miles of jogging on the beach, we were ready for the Tahoe adventure.

David Travels uses Delta Airlines out of Miami. We checked our four bags and three pair of skis with a Red Cap on the sidewalk before even entering the airline building and did not see them again until they were delivered to our room at the Cal-Neva lodge in Lake Tahoe. This convenience alone spoke well for the trip organizers! A clearly printed itinerary was passed to each traveler and before long we were on our way. At Reno, we got our first visual thrill as we stepped off the plane. The Delta aircraft stopped well away from the passenger building and this allowed us to drink in a startling panorama, as the airport is surrounded by snow striped

mountains which looked like whipped cream spilling out of the elongated belly of a cold front headed east. A comfortable bus was waiting, and it was a relief to not have to worry about our luggage. The bus ride was a thrilling climb up the old Donner Trail with steep rising mountains on both sides which were dotted with brown cedar and pine. Snow was sprinkled on the north slopes. This part of the tour was reminiscent of the rail trip toward Zermatt in Switzerland. Beautiful. The driver advised us that the land is currently selling at a minimum of $40,000 per acre with $20 a foot being charged to drill for water. Driving through Truckee, the oldest city in the state of California, we noticed a weathered sign on the side of the Hotel Rex, Rooms $1. At Truckee we swung left and headed toward the 8600-foot ski area known as Northstar-at-Tahoe. Suddenly, the first glimpse of the lake—an intense purple blue basin, crystal clear and interrupted only by sporadic whitecaps churned up by a gentle breeze. Cal-Neva Lodge is near Kings Beach, a short peninsula that boldly dents the lake. I have shifted my writing pad to the window now to drink up the beautiful sunrise which has announced itself with gold lined crimson clouds stretched flat across the sky from Incline, another ski area at the left of our window. Incline is all the way beyond Heavenly Valley, the 10,167-foot mammoth ski area south of the lake which peaks above tree line. The hemline of this grand panorama is Lake Tahoe, surely one of the most beautiful natural phenomenons. Six major ski areas surround the lake. My wife and daughter have awakened to join me as we watch the sun climb. We will ski Incline to see what it provides for beginner and novice skiers.
Tuesday, sunrise.

We had a great day at Incline. Super skiers might refer to the area as a golf course, but its paucity of expert runs is made up for with finely manicured terrain for beginner to intermediate skiers and spectacular scenery. Sensibly, the beginner area is a completely separate long slope with just enough of a grade to barely move and it is serviced by its own chair lift! An excellent ski school gets novices off to a good start. The novice runs are also long and wide, and the intermediate terrain has a few short pitches which really stretch the grade of *intermediate* to its highest limit. The view of the lake beneath majestic mountain peaks from almost every slope is truly breathtaking. Advanced skiers who look down their noses at small areas like Incline are cheating themselves of a most beautiful visual experience. I gave a few lessons to our friends and soon was bird-dogged by an Incline instructor who questioned my wife about my identity. Most ski areas frown upon underground instructors using their slopes. In this case, the instructor turned out to be the Incline Ski School Director who was understanding and most generous as he agreed to let me teach but requested that our group not line up as a class. The lessons that followed had to be semi-private, which our friends didn't seem to mind at all. Today, we will try Squaw Valley, a half hour drive away.
Tuesday, 9 PM.

I can't wait until tomorrow's sunrise to tell you about the thrill of discovering the magnificent, awesome, sparsely treed ski area called Squaw Valley. David Travels arranged for van service from Cal-Neva to the mountain at 8 and 10 AM. We opted for a rented car. Famed for its selection

Squaw Valley is expansive. This peak supports the gondola terminal. That ball in the upper right is a gondola on its way up.

riding high altitude chairlifts, then ride the gondola or tram back down at the end of the day! Bolder low intermediates ski down to the base elevation meeting few obstacles during their gently sloping 2,000-foot descent. Squaw is one of the few major ski areas which offers ski school classes that begin *at the top,* so students don't have to spend half their lesson riding a lift! To call Squaw big is an understatement. It boasts five soaring High Sierra peaks—Red-Dog, KT-22, Squaw Peak, Emigrant and Granite Chief. Many of the runs from the peaks drop from cornices and challenging headwalls, super steep and super moguled, with the bumps looking like huge blankets of inverted egg cartons, daring the most confident of skiers to make it without a fall to the more gently sloping gullies which funnel toward the valley. It takes a pretty good skier to be able to ski every run at Squaw in a day. With all it has to offer (and that is quite a bit more than most ski areas) Squaw is the most generous ski area we have found, allowing children under 12 to *ski free* when accompanied by a parent on a fully paid day ticket which sells for $15. Another super bonus is that day tickets if they are turned in before noon get a refund of $6!

Incidentally, I still can't believe it, but do you know that a week of ski lift tickets were included in the David Travels package and may be used for any of the six major ski areas which surround the lake? This even beats the four mountain reciprocal at Aspen! David Travels took care of *all* the red tape. Our lift tickets were waiting in an envelope with our room keys and a ski area bus pass when we checked into the Cal-Neva Lodge. Are you still wondering if a ski tour is for you? Here's something else to chew on: The check out sign on the back of our door reads $56 per day. While David Travels probably was offered a substantial reduction of that rate in exchange for filling a couple of floors of rooms, the posted price should give you an idea of the quality of the rooms. I know for a fact that Marge and I could not possibly afford to spend that kind of money on a privately arranged ski tour trip!

as a site for the 8th Olympic Winter Games in 1960, Squaw is now what might be called a World-Class ski area, as its 25 lifts and spacious slopes of every conceivable grade cater to skiers of every proficiency level. Following the lead of many European ski areas, novice to low intermediate slopes have been designed close to the peaks at 8200 feet. Intrepid skiers ride the gondola or tram to their ballroom slopes, ski there all day

The moguls of KT-22 at Squaw will give you goose bumps.

(Above) At Incline and Northstar the ski terrain is not unlike many ski areas in the northeast, but the cedars and pines are much taller.

(Right) Cami Covino carves a neat turn at Northstar. It was warm enough to ski in just a wind shirt!

Sunrise, Thursday

The elevation of Northstar fooled us. We expected an exciting mountain with precipitous drops, but were greeted by a beautifully designed novice to intermediate area, heavily treed with meticulously manicured slopes not unlike many ski areas back east. Condominiums closely bordered the lower lift lines, and there was a *very* friendly atmosphere. Californians, we have noted, go all out for the purchase of expensive colorful ski outfits, in some cases exceeding the cost of their skis and boots! Many of the stretch pants on the attractive women looked as though they were painted on, but most notable are the colorful, clear complexions and well conditioned bodies of either sex among the native California skiers we have seen. The local newspapers give a clue to their natural life-style; almost every page is bordered with ads for running shoes, paddle board courts, ski areas, health clubs, health foods, etc. I counted nine articles in today's paper announcing different foot races for participants of all ages. It would appear that this healthy contingent of California residents has caught up with and surpassed the dopers and sexual deviates which seem to have received more press in the newspapers across the country over the past few decades. At any rate, the jovial, refreshing and gregarious scene at Northstar must be good PR, because this area, which boasts no great view of the lake nor the mountains, and has no truly expert slopes, save about 50 feet of the lift line run from the top, is one of the most popular ski areas that surround the lake. It is so popular, in fact, that they close their ticket windows when 4,000 lift tickets have been sold, sometimes as early as 8:30 AM on a weekend!

Our day was sunny and warm enough to ski in a sweater. I even noticed some shorts and gloveless hands. One skier who looked like Dolly Parton did a neat bouncing number in just a thin turtleneck to the joy of we fortunate voyeurs on the lift above her. Neat! We topped off our day with a fantastic meal at Le Cheminee, a cozy, delightful French restaurant just down the road. Ski clothes were permitted. Tonight, many of the David Travels night trippers will challenge the vast Casino on the first floor of the Cal-Neva. Some of them try their luck well thru every night, as the gambling tables are open 24 hours round the clock! Of course, that part of the group doesn't ski.

Thursday, 8:30 PM.

Bumps. Thousands of squirrely skier built moguls. Some steep and menacing. Some round, wide and friendly. Some began just 10 feet below a cornice on a headwall of 60 degrees. Not reserved for a few expert slopes; not waiting to be

The most beautiful sight during our exciting week at Lake Tahoe was the thrill of watching my daughter's face, enthralled by the western adventure.

chewed up by some tank treaded snow cat. Just honest to goodness that's-what-skiing-used-to-be-like *bumps*. Alpine Meadows is *loaded* with them; they literally blanket over two thirds of the bowl wherever the trees are sparse. And they are indeed sparse at Alpine. The trails have no boundaries as they blend into one another offering western skiing at its very best. Today, every other ski area surrounding Lake Tahoe was whipped with violent winds. Precious powder was swept off the slopes and into the forest or into giant drifts that kept changing. At Alpine Meadows we could see snow rising upward around the whole perimeter of the bowl, then curling and spilling like a monstrous wave as it covered the upper slopes like an avalanche. "There's always powder here," confided an affable local. "If it is not fresh, it's old snow that has been shaved off the other side by the winds and dumped into our Meadows!" Much of the upper area reminded me of another skier's heaven, Taos, in New Mexico, but Alpine has more wide mogul fields. Both areas have a long ridge at the summit from which you can choose any line of descent. This is almost wilderness skiing, and at Alpine none of it is marked out of bounds! Here and there you will find signs that say, "Cliff" or "Slow Down," and some of the peaks are avalanche prone. But the ski patrol is very efficient. Every time I sat beside a shade giving cedar to change my film, a patrolman would appear, from out of nowhere, it seemed, to ask if I was having trouble! At Alpine, the grades are less steep but wide and more mogul populated. Nice bumps. The kind that keep you pumping, but which are spaced well enough for smooth carving and an occasional jump. We giggled, hooted and snarled our way down with much less fear and hesitation than we experienced on KT-22 at Squaw. Real skiing!

I can't say enough about this spacious beautiful ski area. Many locals will feel sad that I have said as much as I have; they would like to keep Alpine Meadows to themselves. Free daily shuttle buses ferry skiers from the Cal-Neva Lodge and from all points around the lake, and the bus will pick up anyone who waves it down along its route. There is a convenient Day School at the base where you can drop off preskiers, and this is the first ski area we have visited around the lake where the food fare was more than cooked and packaged hamburgers and franks. Attractive ski hostesses, wearing banners which introduce themselves, ski all over the mountain to assist skiers who are new to the mountain. Pretty girls seem to be quite common at all the ski areas around the lake. It is a singles' Paradise, but you better know how to ski!

Saturday, sunrise

Strong winds raped the best of the High Sierra ski areas, stripping them of the little cover they had after 2 weeks of no new snow. The boiler plate and ice that is left is not new to this eastern skier, but we dropped our original plan to ski Heavenly Valley and opted for Northstar yesterday, where heavy tree population has tempered the winds and some powder still manages to survive above a dangerously shallow base on most of the trails. By today nicknames have developed for the principal group I have been teaching—"Haystack" for Louis, whose bib warm-up suit is a bit oversized; "Moan" and "Groan" for Steve and another Steve, two defense attorneys who apparently dislike even minor discomforts; "Mingo" for Bill, short for Flamingo, after the size of his legs; and "Flintstone" for Fred, who is a bit thick in the middle. It is amazing how few of the rest of the huge group we have even seen. I had visions of traveling from the ski areas to dinner and apreès ski activities with the entire contingent of close to 100. I have always thought group trips to be like that. Not so with David Travels. You can be as free and individual as you care to be. My impression of the group experience has changed.

The week has flown, but we sure made the most of it. Lucking out on the weather, we avoided a brutal storm system which stretched clear across the northern states all week. Our home in Vermont must look like an igloo. We are all tanned as leather from a week of fast skiing and lots of sun. Some of our group won over $1500 in the Cal-Neva Casino. A few lost twice that much. It has been a perfect vacation, which I thought we should tell you about, as it might encourage you to try the surprisingly hassleless group experience. David Travels is located at 1175 N.E. 125 Street, North Miami, Florida 33161. Their phone number is 800-327-0196. We are planning to book with them again in February 1980. Join us!